The Spirit of
LEADERSHIP

The Spirit of
LEADERSHIP

Liberating the Leader
in Each of Us

HARRISON OWEN

Berrett-Koehler Publishers, Inc.
San Francisco

Berrett-Koehler Publishers, Inc.
235 Montgomery Street, Suite 650
San Francisco, CA 94104-2916
Tel.: (415) 288-0260   Fax: (415) 362-2512
www.bkconnection.com

ORDERING INFORMATION

Individual sales. Berrett-Koehler publications are available through most bookstores. They can also be ordered direct from Berrett-Koehler at the address above.

Quantity sales. Special discounts are available on quantity purchases by corporations, associations, and others. For details, contact the Special Sales Department of Berrett-Koehler at the address above.

Orders for college textbook/course adoption use. Please contact Berrett-Koehler Publishers at the address above.

Orders by U.S. trade bookstores and wholesalers. Please contact Publishers Group West, 1700 Fourth Street, Berkeley, CA 94710. Tel: (510) 528-1444; fax: (510) 528-3444.

Printed in the United States of America.

Library of Congress Cataloging-in-Publication Data

Owen, Harrison. 1935–
   The spirit of leadership : liberating the leader in each of us / Harrison Owen.
      p.   cm.
   Rev. ed. of: Leadership is. 1990
   Includes bibliographical references and index.
   ISBN-10: 1-57675-056-6; ISBN-13:978-1-57675-056-8 (alk. paper)
   1. Leadership.   I. Owen, Harrison, 1935–   Leadership is.
II. Title
HD57.7.O94 1999
658.4'09—dc21   99-11598

First Edition
06 digital

Interior design and composition by Beverly Butterfield.

CONTENTS

PREFACE

This book was written in 1989 and originally published by Abbott Publishing in 1990. It is amazing to me how much has happened to our world and our species since that time. But despite the almost cataclysmic changes that have occurred, I believe that the essential message of the book remains valid: we are in the midst of transformation, and leadership, along with everything else in our lives, has become or must become something quite different from what it has been.

Thanks to Steve Piersanti and all the good folks at Berrett-Koehler, this book is now available more broadly. I hope that you, as part of that broader audience, will enjoy reading it even as others apparently have enjoyed it before you. For myself, preparing the manuscript has been a remarkable experience in revisiting some old places and seeing them with new eyes.

HARRISON OWEN
Potomac, Maryland
January 1999

CHAPTER I

Where Have All the Leaders Gone?

"Where have all the leaders gone?" That could well be the song for the last part of the twentieth century. In the national press, scarcely a day passes without extended discussion of the lack of political leadership and the apparent inability of the major political parties to raise up anyone who remotely looks the part.

Corporate America is in little better shape. The strong, charismatic, decisive leader of yesteryear has seemingly been replaced by colorless men. Bold strokes have given way to defensive strategies, aimed less at defining the future than at preserving the past.

Indeed, to the extent that heroes and leaders of the people still populate the planet—at least the U.S. portion of the planet—as likely as not, they appear to be rogues: the corporate raiders and other folks who live by the Darwinian law of survival. Brandishing their leveraged buyouts, they add another notch to their guns.

As we sing our song and look for leaders, we find vast numbers of willing guides and commentators. Books and courses on leaders and leadership seem to have risen in inverse proportion to our perception of available talent. We are counseled on how to take charge, be assertive, and don the charismatic cloak, and other surefire methods for slaying dragons and summoning popular support. But for all the courses and training time, it seems that the refrain is still to be sung, "Where have all the leaders gone?"

The current crisis in leadership is genuine, but its cause may be more a matter of our perception. There is no question that leaders of the kind we have always known are in short supply. We might ask whether something has gone wrong with the genetic pool such that *Homo sapiens* no longer possesses the capacity to lead. Or could it be that the times have changed and leadership "as it used to be" is no longer appropriate?

Here is my theory. As the structures of our world and the conditions of certainty have yielded to an avalanche of change, the extent of our longing for stable, definitive leadership has been exceeded only by the impossibility of finding it. The fault lies not with leadership but rather with ourselves and our expectations. In the old days, leaders were supposed to make sense of chaos, to make certainty of doubt, and to create positive action plans for the resolution of imponderable paradoxes. Good leaders straightened things out. Should chaos rear its ugly head, the leader was expected to restore normality immediately.

But there's the rub. Chaos is now considered normal, paradoxes cannot be resolved, and certainty is possible only to the level of high probability. Leadership that attempts to deliver in terms of fixing any of this can only fail. And that is exactly what is happening.

Have the Leaders Really Gone?

Now, suppose we were to twist things around a bit, even at the risk of charges of Pollyannaism. As strange as our world appears at the moment, and despite all the obvious risks now present, isn't it quite remarkable that we appear to be muddling through as well as we are? To the extent that leadership is necessary to survival, perhaps leadership is not as absent as we have thought.

The list of impending disasters, potential and actual, is long: nuclear holocaust, acid rain, holes in the ozone layer, overpopulation, famine, chemical wastes, the greenhouse effect, omnipresent carcinogens, and a variety of other planetary catastrophes. At the level of the marketplace, we confront such difficulties as financial collapse, monumental national debt, plant closings, downsizing, restructuring, takeovers, and the elimination of entire industries. Were one given to pessimism, there is enough material here to legitimize a massive state of depression. Yet for all that is going wrong, will go wrong, or could go wrong, the fact remains that we seem to be making it, one way or another. Much like Mark Twain said, we may remark that the report of our imminent demise is premature. And to the extent that leadership is now, as always, necessary for our survival, one might suspect that it is still present somehow.

Obviously *Homo sapiens,* and indeed the small planet Earth, could cease to exist tomorrow morning, or sooner. But that has always been true, if not for reasons of our own stupidity, then because of some aberrant asteroid. Yet for several billion years planet Earth and its passengers have survived, one might say prospered. Contrary to every prediction of disaster to date, we are still here. What on Earth, we may ask, is going on? What would we be doing if we thought what we were doing made sense?

What on Earth Is Going On?

We are doing what we've always done: we are transforming. In one way or another, with or without our permission, we are headed down the path we have always been meant to follow— toward the fulfillment of our human potential. There is, of course, no guarantee that we are finally going to make it.

The process of transformation is not always pleasant; indeed, it can be downright terrifying. For transformation means that the old forms of our existence are blown apart and put aside, creating open space within which a new expression of us may emerge. For those who have found their meaning exclusively in the forms and structures of life, the experience is actually beyond terror, for it appears that life itself is about to cease. And in truth, life as it was does come to an end. That is chaos, but it may also be the nutrient seedbed from which new life will emerge.

And what of leadership? Two versions of the leadership tale are currently told. The first version is one we have been telling for some time, in which the few, or even "The One," have all the answers, and therefore the power, to protect us from chaos. Because of their strength, we learn, or are forced, to do *the right thing* that will ensure the preservation of life as we have come to expect it. Order and stability are the fruits of our obedience, and a full belly, a full garage, and lifetime employment are the anticipated rewards. And when, at a time such as now, order and stability are mostly apparent in their absence, we look around for some suitable object of blame. That blame object is not far away: there is a lack of leadership. If that were not true, so goes the story, things would obviously be better than they are. Perhaps.

But there is another story, in which leadership is not the exclusive property of the few or The One. Questions, not answers, predominate, and the right thing is no *thing* at all. In this story, there is no lack of leadership, but rather the emergent presence of a very different sort of leadership. It is new, really there, and really effective. Leadership under the conditions of transformation is a collective and constantly redistributed function, and not the private property of the few or The One. The role of leadership is to engage in the quest (to pose the question) for the realization of human potential. And the goal of leadership is not the establishment of some perfect state (the right thing), but rather the heightened quality of the journey itself. The secret is out. We are all leaders, and there are plenty of us—at least according to this story.

A Word About Storytelling and the Teller of This Tale

Stories and the telling of them have, until quite recently, occupied a place of honor in society. But somehow we became infatuated with the facts, nothing but the facts, and stories are sometimes notably short on such vital details. As for storytellers, they are simply not to be trusted with the task of presenting reality with starkest objectivity. All of these allegations and suspicions are true with regard to this book. It is a story and I am a storyteller.

There is, however, a possibly deeper way of looking at the enterprise of storytelling. The intent is not so much to render "the Truth" in literal, factual detail, but rather to create the conditions under which the Truth may be perceived. Storytelling, in short, is a collaborative undertaking between the teller of the tale and the hearer (or in this case, the reader). When the storyteller does the job well, he or she creates an environment in which the Truth appears, less by the massive assemblage of fact and logical argument than by creating a resonant field wherein the hearer's imagination and life experience may grow and in this case call forth a useful understanding of leadership. So, if you are anticipating a careful review of all the available literature, combined with a detailed analysis of the pertinent facts—past, present, and future—you will do well to stop right where you are. This book is not for you.

On the other hand, if you are willing to engage with me in a quest of sorts, to explore some possibly strange spaces and places, we may together develop an understanding of leadership that is powerful and effective for the present day. There are no guarantees, of course, and you will have to judge the extent to which I live up to the standards of the storyteller's trade. But that is the intent. As I said, I am a storyteller. You may determine whether I am a good one.

Of course there are sources for this tale, and the thoughts of others have had their impact, which I will acknowledge as appropriate. But at the end of the day, I alone take responsibility for the integrity of my tale (for better or worse).

The primary source for this story is my own experience, which it may be relevant to share briefly. I am an Anglican (Episcopalian) priest, although it was never my intent to be a parish priest. I was going to be an academic with a fundamental focus on the myth and ritual of the ancient Near East, combined with a fascination with the process of creation as it danced between order and chaos. Season well with a heavy dose of epistemology, the study of how we know, and you have the ingredients for a very esoteric career. But life has a funny way of not working out as you planned. In fact, I have pursued all of these passions for almost forty years, but rarely in the academic environment I had expected.

The halls of the academy gave way to the streets when the civil rights movement erupted in the 1960s. My avocation became a job when I became the executive director of the Adams-Morgan Community Council, a large community action program in Washington, D.C. That job was followed by a stint in West Africa as associate director of Peace Corps/Liberia, doing pretty much the same thing. Upon returning to the United States I became enmeshed in the world of health care as director of a health care infrastructure development program for Long Island, New York. Relatively senior positions with the National Institutes of Health and the Veterans Administration completed my stay in the health care field and also provided my last honest jobs. From 1979 until the present moment I have been—for lack of a better word—a consultant, albeit president of H. H. Owen and Company.

H.H.O. and Company is an enormous operation consisting of me in all roles, with able assistance from my wife, Ethelyn, and our children (occasionally and usually under duress). There has never been a business plan, and marketing efforts have been miserable to nonexistent. In fact, I've never really understood what business I've been in until it has happened. Clarity on the nature of my business is still elusive, but it has definitely been a wonderful ride!

It all began as I sat beneath a cottonwood tree. How is that for the commencement of a tale? In the moment, I felt a profound connection, not only to the tree but also to the earth from which it grew and the sky toward which it pointed—and to the people and places of the earth: organizations and families, nations and businesses, dogs, cats, and all the wild creatures connected by and through what I could only call *Spirit* with a capital S. The experience was hardly rational and definitely on the scary side. But there it was.

From that day until this, I do not know what Spirit is, and I feel little inclination for precise definition. Perhaps this is laziness, but it feels more like questions of possibility and necessity. No definition seems to work very well, and in the final analysis precise definition is really not needed. Spirit is one of those "things" you know when you run into it, and you know when it is not there. Words fail, as they probably should. Mystery seems to be an essential precondition for the appreciation of Spirit.

It occurred to me at the time that such experiences could well appear weird to many, and something of a mental health hazard to more than a few. Over the years I have been somewhat comforted to find that other folks apparently suffer from similar aberrations. Perhaps there had not been a cottonwood tree in their experience, but it turns out that encounters with Spirit are pretty commonplace. Indeed, I have discovered that from the loading dock to the boardroom, everybody knows when Spirit is up, and also when Spirit has disappeared. Wonderful things seem to happen when Spirit is present, and in its absence nothing much seems to take its place. No amount of money, technology, or brilliant ideas seems to make a difference when Spirit has gone over the hill. Call it lack of inspiration if you like, and *inspiration* after all means to be inspirited.

So, I would guess that my business is all about Spirit. That being the case, it will not surprise you to learn that for me Spirit is the most important thing.

When it comes to leadership, the connection with Spirit is essential. Leadership in the absence of Spirit just does not make it. And Spirit simply refuses to play by somebody else's rules, as in "command and control." It goes its own way, thank you very much. So leadership with Spirit, or spirited leadership, must be something else, having little to do with positional power and authority, which were once considered essential for those who would call themselves leaders.

The connection between leadership and Spirit is much more than an intellectual proposition for me, although it is certainly that. Fundamentally, it is a matter of experience and, if you will, necessity. Although it is true that I have held positions with at least the appearance of formal power and authority attached, I can honestly say that I have never accomplished anything of significance through the use of such authority. There always seemed to be a better and, in many ways, simpler way, which I can call only the way of Spirit. In recent years, this better, simpler way has been the only way. There has quite simply been nothing else available. Formal positional authority does not exist for me, and yet I would like to think that I have manifested leadership in several areas—Organization Transformation and Open Space Technology, to name two—and that the results have been useful.

Organization Transformation

The world of the early 1980s was a curious one indeed. Simultaneously we were visited by Ronald Reagan, Marilyn Ferguson, John Naisbitt, and Tom Peters. Not that these folks did it all by themselves, but they were representative. Reagan gave us a tough-guy conservative in the White House; Ferguson introduced the New Age; Naisbitt pointed out that the world was doing very strange things, which he called *transformation*; and Peters told great stories about something we had almost lost sight of—excellence. For me and a handful of close friends and colleagues, the times were pregnant indeed.

In our part of the world we had noticed that the organizations with which we worked, typically as consultants, were behaving in a very odd manner. Instead of following nice, orderly developmental patterns, they seemed to be taking discontinuous jumps. It was pretty messy and often painful for everybody involved.

A friend, David BelleIsle (then at Martin Marrieta), and I compared notes, and six months' dialogue convinced us that a major part of our personal difficulty was that we were looking at a new (for us) reality through old eyes. We expected development (as in Organization Development), but what we were witnessing was transformation, and frankly we did not have a clue to what was really going on.

Our ignorance precipitated an effort to sketch out a phenomenology of transformation in organizations, and in the spring of 1982 we presented a paper at a regional meeting of the Organization Development Network. The wisdom of hindsight shows clearly that this was a very rough effort, but it created a spark— especially a small throwaway comment at the conclusion, in which I said something like "Organization Development has been an extraordinarily useful approach until now, but it would seem that in the days of the Third Wave1 we may need a different way of looking at things, which we would call Organization Transformation. Frankly, we have no clear idea what this new approach might look like,[2] but if any of you are interested in figuring it out, please let us know."

To be honest, I anticipated no response. How wrong I was. One year later, 250 people from all over the world showed up for the First International Symposium on Organization Transformation (OT1). We had no official sponsorship, primarily because we did not think we could get it and did not have the interest and energy to try. In 1998 we convened OT16, which now takes place in multiple locations in the United States and Europe. There is still no official sponsorship—indeed, there are no continuing organization, membership, or bylaws, or even a bank account. The impact, however, has definitely been more than nothing. The once-ethereal words *Organization Transformation* can now be found with regularity in such mainstream publications as the *Wall Street Journal* and the *New York Times.* It is possible to receive a degree in Organization Transformation, although I am not quite sure why one would want to do that. Last but not least, I have discovered that the IBM Consulting Group has a special practice that they call Organization Transformation, and they are not alone. Things are surely different than they were in 1982.

And what does all this have to do with leadership and Spirit? Everything, I think. Without a shred of formal authority and no organizational backing, a very small group of folks opened some new space in which the Spirit of a much larger group of folks showed up. The results speak for themselves. That is what I call *leadership.*

Open Space Technology

Open Space Technology (OST) is, at the very least, a deceptively simple approach to better, more productive meetings in which groups of from five to one thousand people quickly self-organize to deal effectively with complex issues in a very short time.[3] The genesis of OST had little to do with careful design and a complete review of the available literature. It happened when, at the conclusion of OT1, it became clear to me and most other folks who attended that the really exciting stuff had all happened during the coffee breaks. Because I had devoted a year, almost full-time, to endless committee meetings designed to arrange all the details of speakers and panels, this realization came as something of a shock. Clearly what everybody truly liked was the one thing I'd had nothing to do with. There had to be a better way.

Inspiration for the better way came from my experience in Liberia, West Africa, particularly in a small town called Balamah. In Balamah, and traditional villages everywhere, everything of importance takes place in a circle. The elders meet in a circle, disputes are settled in a circle, the people dance in a circle, the villages are constructed in a circle (roughly), and there is always an open space in the center. My thought was, if we could invite meeting participants to gather in a circle, amazing things might happen. Add a few simple elements, such as a bulletin board (to identify issues for discussion) and a marketplace (in which to arrange the details of time and space), and perhaps all that planning I had suffered through could be eliminated.

Subsequent experience around the world has demonstrated that the folks of Balamah had it right. Hundreds of thousands of people from every walk of life and from every continent on the planet have met in Open Space. And it always seems to work. Amazing things do happen.

For purposes of the discussion of leadership and Spirit, two lessons have been important. The first lesson has been the rapid dissemination of OST, and the second has been the role of the facilitator.

THE SPREAD OF OST

OST has always been an organizational orphan. Institutional sponsorship has been zero, and nothing approaching a marketing plan, to say nothing of the necessary financial resources to support such a thing, has ever existed. But in a very short time, OST has gone around the world.

Had all of this been run as a proper business, with franchises and some form of central control, the current operation would certainly have achieved multimillion-dollar status. Every year a dozen or so training programs are offered in the United States, Canada, and Europe, with seven hunded current graduates. Add in one thousand to three thousand additional practitioners (rough estimate) whose formal introduction to the process may have been as a participant, or perhaps reading the book, and you have a fairly major operation. It all began in Balamah, and some would say that I am responsible for the lot.

To deny my pride in the accomplishment to date would be foolish, but none of it occurred as some textbooks on leadership and management dictate. Centralized control, positional power, formal communication, and tight organizational structure have never been part of the picture. Indeed, any sense of control that I might once have thought I possessed has long since disappeared. From the beginning this has been an out-of-control operation, which (in my judgment) is precisely why it has succeeded so handsomely.

Seen from the inside, my role as leader has been nothing more than to open space so that Spirit can show up. And the Spirit of a lot of folks has indeed shown up, producing a global collaborative effort as all of us have sought to understand and enhance the amazing things that are happening in Open Space. I am clear that OST is not in any sense my property. It is free for the taking, and many people have done just that. Nor is it my invention, for literally thousands of people have had a significant hand in its development. Actually, if anybody deserves all the credit, it is the good people of Balamah. After all, they were there first.

THE OPEN SPACE FACILITATOR

Ever since the first Open Space, which occurred in 1985, each event has become a natural laboratory in which to observe the remarkable potential of humankind coming into fullness. Amazing things do happen, with regularity. Complex designs for multimillion-dollar projects that were estimated to take ten months get done in two days. Deeply conflicted groups find a way to commonality, resulting in substantive resolution of long-standing difficulties, and more. As surprising as such outcomes may be, the manner in which they are achieved is even more surprising. Absolutely no up-front planning takes place, yet a complex meeting agenda appears in less than an hour. No training of participants ever happens, and yet they demonstratively function well as self-managed work teams. Most remarkably, no facilitator intervenes in any session; indeed, with the exception of a brief appearance at the very beginning, the facilitator is most notable by his or her absence.

The strange behavior of the Open Space facilitator is definitely an anomaly, at least a far as current group process management practice is concerned, but I believe there may be more going on here than meets the eye. In fact, the Open Space facilitator does two, but only two, very important things. He or she *opens space* and then *holds space.*

Opening space occurs at the beginning when the theme is announced and the participants are invited to identify all of the issues and opportunities of concern to them that they would care to address during the course of the gathering. Rarely does this activity take longer than fifteen to twenty minutes, and it is followed by what sometimes turns into a major rush as participants crowd the central open space to announce their individual areas of concern, and to post on the wall of the conference room—which quickly becomes the community bulletin board—the subject, time, and place of their sessions. I am not quite sure how you would characterize such a happening, but for me, standing in the center of the circle, it is quite clear that Spirit has shown up.

The second function of the facilitator, holding space, starts the moment the people move to claim the space. The observable role of the facilitator quickly passes from single speaker standing in the center of the circle to "microphone stand"—holding the microphone so that the participants can make their announcements. And when the announcements have all been made and the sessions have been posted, there is nothing more for the facilitator to do. In my case, I leave the room, and very often I go and take a nap.

Upon my return, and for the duration of the gathering, my level of doing can usually be measured in minus quantities, limited to such things as picking up trash and stray coffee cups. Open Space, after all, is an extended coffee break. But if my doing is limited, my being (present) is a full-time occupation.

My job is to preserve the safety (sanctity?) of the space so that the Spirit of the participants can keep showing up and get the job (whatever that might be) done. A technical term, *witness*, usually found in esoteric literature, captures pretty closely what transpires. It is all about supportive presence, which apparently does little but "be's" a lot.

The concern here is not with the details of Open Space facilitation, but if your curiosity has been piqued I invite you to try a little Open Space,[4] maybe with the help of *The User's Guide*, mentioned in note 3. The concern is leadership and Spirit, and I sincerely believe that the experience that I and countless others have had in the role of Open Space facilitator can well be instructive, and possibly paradigmatic, of what I understand leadership to be all about. Briefly said, leadership opens the space for Spirit to show up, and then leadership keeps that space open so that the job gets done. Call it inspiration.

Coming Attractions

So much for introductions of myself and the subject matter at hand. The following itinerary outlines the journey ahead in order to give you a taste of coming attractions.

I begin in Chapter Two with a brief consideration of the current context in which leadership must function, which quite simply is our transforming world. Not long ago it appeared necessary to adduce many facts and arguments to buttress the notion that transformation is a present happening. That now seems like a total waste of time, for unless you are very insensitive or living on a different planet, the morning news should make the point.

With the context established, I take a look in Chapter Three at the new rules of leadership, rules appropriate to the very different ball game we now find ourselves playing. As it turns out, the rules are not so much new as surprising, for they are in fact the old, old rules we have always played by in the informal organization.

Chapter Four goes somewhat deeper as I address some new lessons learned from those who have always played far from the levers of formal power and authority—the disenfranchised, particularly women. Lacking a definitive study of effective female strategies under the conditions of radical disenfranchisement, I turn to close personal experiences with my mother and her friends.

Then, it is on to the heart of the matter, in Chapters Five and Six, with the perhaps outrageous suggestion that leadership in its essence is our link to the deep, primal forces symbolized by the Dragon. Somewhere in the underground we connect with the true source of Leadership—that is, Spirit.

With the proper domain of leadership identified, I then consider five functions of leadership within that domain:

- To evoke Spirit through vision (Chapter Seven)
- To grow Spirit through collective storytelling (Chapter Eight)
- To sustain Spirit through structure (Chapter Nine)
- To comfort Spirit when things fall apart (Chapter Ten)
- To raise Spirit, thereby enabling the conditions of renewal (Chapter Eleven)

Chapter Twelve brings us to the end of the tale with some concluding thoughts on the Spirit of leadership or, more particularly, the leader's Spirit. The leadership role is available to us all, and assuming that role in any circumstances in which we find ourselves may well turn out to be the defining moment (or moments) of our humanity. But it is also demanding work, not to be taken on lightly or taken without support and preparation.

NOTES

1. Alvin Toffler had just published *The Third Wave*.
2. If you are interested in where I came out in an understanding of Organization Transformation, consult my book *Spirit: Transformation and Development in Organizations* (Potomac, Md.: Abbott, 1987).
3. For the details on what Open Space is, how to create it, and what it might mean, please consult my books *Open Space Technology: A User's Guide* and *Expanding Our Now: The Story of Open Space Technology* (San Francisco: Berrett-Koehler, 1998).
4. A brief note on Open Space and Open Space Technology: Those of you who first encountered my work through experiences with or reading about Open Space Technology may find my use of the words Open Space in this book a trifle confusing. There are many instances of open space, but virtually none of them refer to the meeting methodology. The truth of the matter is that Open Space (for me) was first something approaching a state of being, and only secondarily a way of meeting. The double usage occurred when I noticed that people meeting in the open space of Open Space Technology regularly experienced the state of being that I had called Open Space. Confusing for sure, but probably useful for all of that. If you have never heard of Open Space Technology, you won't be bothered. But if you have, you might want to look again at what is clearly

a useful way to hold meetings. There may be more going on than meets the eye. For starters, I think you will find that leadership in Open Space is the same whether in a meeting or in the open space of our lives.

CHAPTER 2

Transformation

The Context of Leadership

Transformation is occurring now—not later, not soon, but right this instant. Of course it has always been so, for the history of our species has been an ongoing journey of the evolution of consciousness: the continuous transformation of our essence from one form into a new one. From the moment we branched out from our brothers and sisters who constitute the rest of the animal kingdom—indeed, from the moment before that moment, when animal and plant became distinct entities—transformation has been occurring. To tell the truth, it all began, if it began at all, in that fiery instant of pure energy expanding infinitely across nothingness. And who knows, maybe it never began but always was. Whatever the point of genesis, transformation is not new.

What is new, or at least what strikes us as strange, is the *rate* of transformation. There clearly have been times when things seemed never to change. Perhaps appearances were deceiving, or we were deceived by our own lack of awareness, but at times it certainly seemed that yesterday, today, and tomorrow were all of a piece. Our deception was probably self-induced. No one and no thing likes to change, for all systems are essentially conservative. So it may well be that we have played the ancient and honorable game of the emperor's new clothes. Everybody knew the emperor was naked, but no one dared say so.

Regardless of how things have been, they are surely different now. And the excitement and terror of the moment lie less in the actual differences than in the speed with which the differences become manifest. We are riding the tiger to somewhere, and we no longer need the pundits and gurus of this world to tell us so. We need only to get out of bed each morning to see what massive change the rolling forces of transformation have brought to us that day.

In the realm of business, as old ways of doing things are placed at risk, an open space is created in which new ways of being in the marketplace come into existence. Some people, how-ever, will find the challenge of the moment more than they can bear and will seek to deal with the future as they have with the past. In organizational terms, this means that when the fit between corporation and environment is less than comfortable, the tried-and-true answer is to restructure and reorganize. Somewhere, somehow, it is assumed, the perfect structure will be discovered. Its shapes may be circles or squares, matrices or hierarchies, but given time and wisdom, not to mention luck, that structure will come forth. And with reorganization comes a host of other efforts to find a comfortable and workable shape: mergers, acquisitions, downsizing, and redirection.

Such organizational efforts at adaptation appear as a crazy dance. Starting with slow, measured steps, they move toward vio-lently oscillating patterns: centralize, decentralize, network, apply authoritarian control, introduce quality circles, get rid of quality circles, encourage employee participation, run it all from the top.

Just when it seems that there is a momentary respite, and "finally, we can get ourselves organized," some new bolt from the blue crashes through. A corporate raider appears on the hori-zon. The Middle East erupts in chaos, and oil is shut off. Your only product hits number one on the carcinogen list. The market crashes on the day of your big public offering. The Soviet empire falls apart, peace of a sort breaks out, and all your business is in defense. On days like these the word *change* hardly seems big enough, and the thought of managing change is almost laughable, as if anybody could manage the forces we experience. Seems like transformation is here to stay.

The Great Organizational Picture Show

The experience of change is not unlike watching an old motion picture that lurches from frame to frame. Things are moving too fast to catch the details in any single frame, but too slowly and erratically to be comfortable with the flow of motion.

Actually, in the "good old days" we didn't have motion pictures at all; rather, a still shot was projected on the screen for what seemed like forever. The details and relationships were frozen, and we grew very comfortable with the sameness. Then some bright, young fellow introduced motion as an added attraction. He placed the old slide projector on rapid advance and we quickly got the idea that motion was involved. Simultaneously, we began to feel jangled and ill, jumping and bouncing from one slide to the next.

THIS IS CHAOS

It is small comfort, but probably useful, to know that the pattern evidenced here is that displayed by any open system caught in the midst of violent environmental disturbance. According to Ilya Prigogine, who has spent a lifetime studying such things, the system moves further and further out of equilibrium until it either explodes and dissipates or "pops" to a new level of complexity and competence, from which it can successfully deal with the emergent environmental realities.[1] The system turns "every which way but loose" (to borrow the title of an old Clint Eastwood movie), trying all conceivable tricks in its bag, making adjustments, jury-rigging old procedures, desperately attempting to make sense of a world that has gone crazy. In the end it lies exhausted and either retires from the field of battle or realizes that it is not doing something wrong, *it is doing the wrong thing*. You simply can't get there from here.

Prigogine has now been joined by a host of other writers traveling under the name of chaos or complexity theorists. Their theories have been well chronicled by Joseph Gleich[2] in his book *Chaos*. An interesting collection of folks from a multiplicity of fields are helping us to discern the rough hand of chaos resolving into order as the creative process rolls on. No longer a stranger to be mentioned only in a whisper, chaos is our constant companion. Worse yet, it appears that chaos is an essential condition for the progress of life. Eliminating chaos is tantamount to eliminating life. Clearly we live in a different world than we used to, and as Margaret Wheatley, author of *Leadership and the New Science*,[3] helps us to realize, the difference drives right to the heart of how we understand and work with our organizations. Leadership as command and control is defeated before it ever starts by the chaotic conditions of the times combined with the virtually unthinkable complexity of all living systems. And what you cannot comprehend you cannot predict—which is more than sufficient to drive control freaks crazy.

But the news of chaos and complexity theory is really no news at all. For millennia the great traditions of the world have understood that the forces of chaos and order conspire in a great cosmic dance to bring forth all that is. Shiva dances as creator and destroyer. The Tao manifests in the yin and yang of shadow and light, order and destruction. And according to the prophet Isaiah, God said, "I create light and darkness. I create peace and chaos" (Isaiah 45:7). It would seem that it has always been so; it is only that we may have forgotten, or more likely deluded ourselves. But no matter what the source—contemporary chaos theory, the wisdom of the ages, or your own experience when you roll out of bed to face a new round of transformation—the message is clear: things aren't what they used to be, and all signs point to more of the same—that is, to the different. So what are our alternatives?

GETTING UP TO SPEED

The analogy of the motion picture holds some useful clues. Imagine that we are still sitting in the Great Organizational Picture Show, feeling lurched and bounced. A number of us would like to get our hands on that young fellow and make him go back to showing one picture at a time—slowly. Unfortunately, it turns out that he is hiding in the projection booth with the door locked. More than that, he is positively obsessed with the idea of motion and just won't listen to any suggestions about going slower. Suddenly one of our number has a totally crazy idea. If not slower, how about faster? Contrary to everybody's better judgment, the suggestion is passed under the door, and the diabolical speed freak obliges.

At first it seems that our worst fears are realized. As each frame succeeds its predecessor at dizzying speed, we are about to loose it all in a meaningless blur. Then a most remarkable thing occurs. As our eyes tire and we lose the ability to grasp each frame in its discreteness, we are left with only the flow of the moving image. And *voilà*—the motion picture is born.

A silly tale with a major point: life in the Great Organizational Picture Show is possible only when you get up to speed, give up on the details, and go with the flow. For us, and for our organizations, the issue and the strategy is much the same. When the forms and structures of our lives pass with such rapidity as to become a blur, it is essential to make sense of the blur.

Making sense of the blur, or getting past the formal structures of our organizations, is made all the more difficult by virtue of the fact that most of us, at least publicly, act as though there were nothing beyond or beneath these forms. When asked to describe our organization, we typically respond by outlining the organizational chart and rendering the balance sheet. After all, these two items, in one form or another, constitute the so-called hard realities of organizational life. We all know that position is power, and that power is money, and both represent the essence of control. After you have dealt with the chart and the balance sheet, what else is there to say? A great deal, it turns out, though most of it doesn't get printed in the business journals.

Position Power and Budget

Take the whole business of position power. Conventional wisdom says that unless you have your name on the chart at a high level, you simply do not have the power to do anything worthwhile. That is what we *say*. But should we find ourselves off in a private corner, facing the question, How do things *really* get done around here? it turns out that most people never follow the organizational chart, and some folks seem totally unaware that it exists. And strange to say, it is often the latter group that gets the most innovative things accomplished. Glorified by Tom Peters as the "Skunk Works,"[4] these are the people who have found that it is infinitely easier to ask for forgiveness than for permission. So much for the formal organizational structure.[5]

When it comes to the balance sheet and the so-called hard numbers of the bottom line, the official position is much the same: it is not just the most important thing—it is the only thing. After all, it is something you can count, count on, and control. This said, we just might remember the global stock market meltdown that occurred way back on October 19, 1987. On that day we all discovered that money was only what you thought it was, and we thought it was a lot less on October 20 than we had thought it was on October 18. In the United States, we literally disimagined half a trillion dollars in twenty-four hours. It just went *poof*. So, although it remains true that balance sheets are important, and certainly something you can count, it is not necessarily true that they can be counted on to reflect value accurately. Something else is involved, which is the activity of the *valuer*. That is us. When we value things, it is unfortunate but true that our judgment is inevitably subjective. So much for the hard, objective numbers.

It might be said, quite fairly, that I have treated the formal, structural aspects of organizational life with less than due seriousness. But I submit that my treatment of these venerable realities is less severe than the treatment they receive at the hands of the world at large. No comments on my part can possibly place organizational structures in a more tenuous position than the transforming conditions of the world. Like it or not, the organizational chart is definitely in the category of "here today, gone tomorrow." Likewise with the balance sheet. Obviously every organization needs one, but its hardness and objectivity surely must be suspect in the wake of October 19 and similar events.

The point, however, is not to ridicule these organizational necessities, but rather to place them in perspective. As important as they both may be, there are other elements, or realities, in organizational life of equal or greater importance.

Let us suppose, for the moment, that the official position was wrong and that in fact the back corridor conversations had some substance. Thus, the keys to leadership, power, and organizational effectiveness may not lie exclusively, or maybe even primarily, along the lines of formal position and communication, but rather in that wispy area sometimes referred to as the "informal organization," the soft side of things. A shocking suggestion, perhaps, and one that many people might rather overlook, if only because it drives directly toward a very sensitive area. The critical issue is *control*—what is it, and do we really have it? And of course, without control leadership is impossible, at least according to the "old story."

The informal organization appears unmanageable. It always seems to be beyond our control, and therefore we suppress it, at best, or even totally ignore it. But should it turn out that control, as we have come to understand it, is rather like the emperor's clothes (there only because we desperately wish it to be), then we might want to take another look at the informal system.

Mount Tamalpais

I am reminded of a story about running down Mount Tamalpais,[6] the majestic peak lying just across the Golden Gate Bridge from San Francisco. Its upper slopes are a vast meadowland spilling down to the sea. Given a sunny day and the wind in your face, resisting the call to run down the hill is impossible.

On such a day, a young family picnicked at the top, and when they had finished their meal, the open slopes beckoned. At first they ran in circles, enjoying the grass, each other, and the soft earth beneath their feet. But as they ran their random patterns, they coalesced into a joyful group bounding down the hillside. The wind blew their hair and the steepness of the hillside stripped away all effort. Intoxicated by a feeling of virtual free fall, they cast caution to the winds and raced downward. Feet and legs pumped faster than anybody could remember, and the exhilarating joy was something none of them would ever forget.

Suddenly, a collective thought occurred. Their carefree descent was nothing short of mad. There were rocks in that field, and trees at the bottom. One misstep and delirious joy would quickly turn to tragedy.

The immediate response was to stop, but they were well past the point of no return. To stop at that speed was to court disaster.

If stopping was impossible, careful foot placement became a necessity: avoid the rocks and tufts of grass, the gopher holes and other secret hideaways of small animals.

Thoughts of care were right, but also impossible. The speed of descent, to say nothing of eyes filled with wind-born tears, brought vision and thinking to near zero levels. The choice was obvious: there was no choice at all. They were out of control, and any attempt to regain control could only result in disaster.

The story ended happily, for the family made it to the bottom of the field. They had learned a little something about the siren call of Mount Tamalpais; but more than that, they now knew that being in control was letting go.

I suggest that we are all running down Mount Tamalpais. Some of us still think we can stop, or possibly reconfigure the shape of the mountain (create a level playing field). Others are running in absolute terror, sustained only by the hope that the bottom will be reached and the mad flight will come to an end. A few are beginning to suspect that there is no end, and further, that human fulfillment lies not in getting the race over but in running it well.

This latter group contains those strange individuals who had the audacity to propose fixing chaos in the Big Organizational Picture Show with more chaos. Speed up, they said, and they were right. Contrary to the conventional wisdom, and counterintuitive as it might have seemed, sense emerged from nonsense when the discrete bits and pieces disappeared in the blur and meaning emerged in the flow.

Perhaps order and chaos are not opposites but necessary and complementary parts of a continuum, descriptive of the flow of life toward whatever it is about to become. And control is a matter of letting go. Of course, if the leader is always expected to be in control, it is small wonder that leadership is in trouble at the moment. But that is not, as I have said, the only story.

NOTES

1. Ilya Prigogine, *Order Out of Chaos* (New York: Bantam Books, 1984).
2. James Gleich, *Chaos: Making a New Science* (New York: Viking Penguin, 1987).
3. Margaret J. Wheatley, *Leadership and the New Science: Learning About Organization from an Orderly Universe* (San Francisco: Berrett-Koehler, 1994).
4. Tom Peters, *In Search of Excellence: Lessons from America's Best-Run Companies* (New York: Warner Books, 1988).
5. My point is not that structure is not useful but that it is not the only thing, nor the most important thing. Appropriate organizational structure is essential, however. Please see Chapter Nine.
6. This story is not mine, and if I could remember the teller, I would surely credit him or her. It is one of my favorites.

CHAPTER 3

A Whole New Ball Game

Leadership and the Informal Organization

To people nurtured in the business school environment who came of age in traditional Western organizations, the world of the informal organization appears strange indeed. It is counterintuitive and somehow wrong. Even though these same people may admit privately that not much gets done in their organization by following the old organizational chart, this admission often takes on the aspect of a secret confession—for everybody knows that position is power and that the balance sheet rules. That is what it says in all the books, and of course they must be right.

As a matter of fact, the shadow world of the informal organization is often treated as the enemy. After all, it operates like the underground economy—off the books and beyond the control of those who think (or hope) that they are in control. Given the training and predisposition of many managers, the predictable, primary response to this strange beast is either to stamp it out or to bring it under control. Informal communication, for example, is presumed to be bad, therefore the formal reporting structure must be adhered to and enforced. The anticipated alternative is chaos.

If control fails, the next strategy is to downplay the power of the off-the-books way of doing business. So, when the academicians and pundits write books on organizations, 99.9 percent (a very rough figure) of what they say relates to the observable control functions. The informal organization, if mentioned at all, appears only in a footnote.

The last strategy is to ignore the shadow world completely. By pretending that the shadow world just doesn't exist, the notion of formal control is not disturbed.

Given responses such as these, it is not surprising that little is known (officially) about the informal organization, and that little use is made of its possible virtues. In more predictable days, when the formal structures apparently worked quite well, the aforementioned treatment of the informal side of things was not only understandable but probably justified. Things have changed, however, and it is time to take a closer look at what is going on beneath the official surface of our organizations—not with the idea of stamping out this strange presence, but rather to learn how it works and how to use it more effectively.

As a matter of fact, there is a considerable body of experience with the informal side of things, developed over the years by people who were denied access to the formal structures of power. These people include all disenfranchised groups, particularly minorities and women. They also include people who have chosen to work "off the books," as it were, in the world of volunteerism, where the coin of the realm is usually not money and position power, but passion, commitment, and purpose.

New Rules for a New Ball Game

The world of the informal organization is a whole new ball game. What makes it difficult to adjust to is that it rather *looks* like the old ball game. After all, it is the same world, the same organizations, and the same products and services. But appearances can be deceiving.

The relationship between the formal and informal organization, and the difficulties created by the apparent sameness of the

THE NEW RULES

Whoever has the ball is leader.

Never oppose force with force.

Play the whole field.

Cooperate in order to compete.

Honor the opposition.

two are not unlike the relationship between the word *football* used in the United States and the word *football* used elsewhere. In different contexts the same word has radically different meanings. In the United States, *football* is football, and Americans know that what everybody else plays is "only" soccer. The rest of the world has a rather different understanding.

The real difficulty for Americans comes about not just because of the differences but also because of the similarities in these games. They have the same name, and the playing field has the same general size and configuration, roughly one hundred yards long with goals at both ends. The fans and the teams sit in the same places along the sides, and at a quick glance the pattern of play seems rather similar. Of course, each game's ball does look a little odd to the fans of the other game. However, were you to get into a soccer game with the rules of football still in mind, you would be in "deep tapioca" for sure.

Take the whole question of leadership and who's in charge. In American football, command is exercised from the sidelines by the coach, who transmits the plays to the quarterback via the tight end. How different it is with soccer: *whoever has the ball is leader.*

There is a strange corollary to this first leadership rule of soccer: ball hogs die. It is absolutely impossible for one person to lead with the ball all the time. When you are playing a nonstop, forty-minute half, human physiology, no matter what the level of will and determination, simply will not permit a continuous effort on the part of a single person. And should some person be crazy enough to try such a Herculean effort, the net result will be not only total exhaustion for the individual but also defeat for the team. So much for having one powerful leader.

Speaking of power, much official wisdom suggests that when some obstacle presents itself, the best, and some would say the only, way to victory is to concentrate all available forces and charge through. Strategy like that may work in American football, but in soccer it is largely ineffective and generally subject to a penalty call. The basic rule is, *never oppose force with force.* This does not mean that speed, endurance, and best effort are of no account, but simply that it is much smarter to create a strategy that plays to the weak points and depends on speed and deception for effectiveness.

To mount such a nonforce strategy, several other rules must be observed. The first is *play the whole field.* It is, of course, tempting to concentrate only on that which is in front of you. After all, everybody can clearly see the goal at the end of the field. But doing that means that there is only one right way to go—ahead. If the way is blocked, however, and one is observing the cardinal principle of not opposing force with force, it is often necessary to move backward in order to make progress. Thereupon arises the strange phenomenon of watching a team kick the ball back into its own territory. The intuitive American response is to yell, "Stop, the goal lies ahead!" True, but to get there one has to take maximum advantage of available space in order to reset the dynamics of play and create an open space that reveals the path.

The requirement to sense the dynamics of play in order to be able to change them brings to light yet another apparently counterintuitive principle: it is *necessary to cooperate in order to compete.* One cannot stand removed in abstract isolation and effectively monitor the dynamics of play. The game's dynamics are more like a dance in which the partners must mirror one another's moves before anything else can happen.

Along with cooperation comes one more strange element of relatedness: *honor the opposition.* Somewhere along the line it became popular to equate the desire to compete and win with high levels of hostility and anger. It is true that occasionally these emotions can produce momentary bursts of superhuman effort, but they are momentary, and for a game of any duration, this is simply insufficient.

The Big Ball Game

Analogies of all sorts, and sports analogies in particular, are useful only to a point. This short excursion into the world of soccer and football has made clearer some of the ways in which the informal organizational world differs from the formal organizational world, but the analogy is limited. Games, by whatever name, are played under narrowly circumscribed conditions: on a field of a certain size, with a set number of players, for an agreed-upon length of time. Obviously the world at large doesn't work that way. In the Big Ball Game, the number of players, the size of the field, and the length of play are constantly changing. Indeed, the object of play (what it means to win) is not only up for discussion, it is often several different things at the same time. Anything can change at any time, and usually does. Under the circumstances, it is not surprising that we often make the effort to cut the odds in our favor, and to define, albeit arbitrarily, some smaller subset of that total world in which we can set the rules and thereby gain control. Indeed, that is exactly what we have done with all our games and our businesses. To date, this strategy has been reasonably successful, but its success should not blind us to the fact that it is indeed a strategy, and an arbitrary one at that. We confuse, at our peril, the world of our imagination and the world as it is.

As much as we might wish it were not so, the simple truth of the matter is, *none of us ultimately sets the rules*. This is true for the man in the street as well as for those elevated individuals we sometimes refer to as our leaders.

For understandable reasons it is comforting to ascribe to "the Great Leader" the power we don't have—believing, if only for the moment, that although we cannot control our destiny, he or she can control it for us. Truly great leaders understand that ascription of power to be a fond hope, and that they, along with everybody else, are basically out of control. Sometimes, of course, the so-called leaders believe their own press, at which point we are all truly in trouble.

At this juncture, we can certainly benefit from the experience of those who by force of circumstance or choice have always known that they live in a world they do not and cannot control. For lifetimes and centuries, they have had to play by somebody else's rules.

CHAPTER 4

Leadership Lessons from the Disenfranchised

Women

The prototypical disenfranchised group is women. For whatever reasons—and we are now beginning to understand some of them—women have been seen by men, and often by themselves, as on the fringes, and certainly not in charge.

> Making generalizations about women, particularly if you happen to be a man, is dangerous. So it is essential to clarify the basis from which I speak and my perceived right for doing so. I speak as a man observing women in my part of the world. That my observations may be warped and biased is a given. As for my right to speak, I take it as true that all humans are both masculine and feminine. As I have come to explore my own feminine aspect, I find that disenfranchised woman is not simply a phenomenon of the external world. She exists in me as well.

The stereotypical view of women, as I was growing up, is captured exquisitely in the song from *My Fair Lady* in which Henry Higgins, the archetype of all male chauvinists, wonders, "Why can't a woman be more like a man?" Women, it seemed, were bereft of logic and were incapable of making plans or following them through. To the extent that they had a use at all, except as playthings for men, it was to be mothers and caretakers of children. Men, after all, were in charge of the world, and the girls were to be left to girlish things.

How we got to the sorry state represented by this stereotype is something for the psychologists and anthropologists to puzzle through. But that we were there, and still are in many ways, seems beyond dispute. Given such a view of woman, the resulting depravation and sheer loss of available human potential is inevitable, and nothing short of catastrophic. Fortunately, there has been somewhat of a turn, and that turn seems to be accelerating as more and more women assume their rightful position in society. Even the corporate "glass ceiling" seems to be giving a bit, although a number of my women friends have found assent to the executive suite a Pyrrhic victory, and subsequently have gone off to create their own fulfillment. That is the corporate loss, but at least the critical element of choice has been established, no longer constrained by stereotypes. Yet turn or not, the truly amazing fact remains that, even when the stereotype held its greatest power, women, or at least some women, managed quite well in the world. How they did that is the point of interest.

To the best of my knowledge, the definitive study of effective female strategies under the conditions of radical disenfranchisement has yet to be undertaken. When it has been done, I think we will learn that not only have a remarkable group of women accomplished incredible things, but also, and most important for our present situation, we (by which I mean everybody in this transforming world) have a lot to learn from their efforts and strategies. Failing such a definitive study, I must rely on what some might term anecdotal evidence—a lifelong, close encounter with a most remarkable group of women: my mother and her friends.

Mother was born at the turn of the century, into a world that was anything but hospitable to a bright, precocious young female. Going to school was allowed, but nobody expected it to amount to much, except as it might better prepare a young lady to assume her proper place in life, as the wife of a proper gentleman. College, or anything beyond that, was generally speaking simply not done.

Mother, it seemed, hadn't read the rule book. Not only did she go to college, but she also continued on for a graduate degree in English. Degrees in hand, she set forth for the world of work, eventually landing a job with a large New York publisher as an assistant editor. Her authors ranked among the best known of the time, and from the little that I know, she was respected in her work and enjoyed it immensely.

Then, for reasons unknown, she left that world and followed a path much more to the liking of those who judge such things. She got married. How or why all of that came to be, I haven't a clue. I do know that Mother's relationship to my father lasted only long enough for my conception and birth. And then she was on her own again.

Being on her own was not to be equated with being alone, for in fact she had a large circle of women friends, and I suppose some men friends as well, although they were never much in evidence. Mother and her friends maintained close contact year-round, but the center of their relatedness was in Maine, where she and I spent all our summers.

Mother's Maine house was her special world, populated exclusively by women. Although it was a strange world for a small boy to grow up in, it was fascinating in a variety of ways, most of which were related to Mother's friends and guests. Over the summers there was a succession of extraordinary women: concert pianists, world class athletes, folks from the world of business and academe. The conversation was civil and urbane, often joyful, and sometimes rational to a fault. And for sure, it bore no relationship to the stereotypical image of the empty-headed woman lamented by Henry Higgins. It seemed idyllic to me then, and in retrospect it appears as a feminine retreat, an isolated place and time where being female was no disadvantage.

Maine was a special place, but more interesting for our present discussion were mother's operations in the larger world. Although she never returned to work in a traditional sense, she was not without a lengthy list of good things to be done: Red Cross drives to organize, blood donor campaigns, fundraising events for the symphony orchestra, and church activities. Actually, her priorities were, in order of importance, the church and a few other things. Like many women before her and since, Mother discovered the church as a place where she could use her considerable talents. But unlike a lot of those women, she refused to remain in that narrow area known as woman's work. In fact, she demonstrated a disconcerting tendency for showing up in any number of places clearly labeled "men only," particularly the vestry.

The vestry was the governing body of the local Episcopal church, and for as long as anybody could remember it had been the private preserve of men, so much so that *vestry* and *vestrymen* were synonymous. Mother changed all that. She became the first *vestryperson.*

I had many opportunities to watch Mother in operation, but how she did what she did as well as she did remained a mystery to me for some time. There was no question that she was effective, and that the things she set her sights on largely came to pass; but how she pulled it all off escaped me.

When she conversed with her male peers and colleagues, it sometimes seemed to me that she had totally lost her capacity for reason. She would begin with one point, leap to another, fall into inexplicable silence, only to reemerge from a totally unpredictable and apparently unrelated quarter. At times she appeared the quintessential scatterbrained woman. Yet I knew this lady to be the same one who could pursue a topic with single-minded rationality among her friends in Maine. But what I first took to be an obvious lapse of sense later emerged as careful strategy. Mother knew what she was doing.

Although she was never afraid to lead, in the traditional sense of that word, she also had a clear sense of her own limitations and endurance. Practically, this meant that she was constantly identifying coleaders and incessantly passing the ball off to them. Just about the time that the opposition (usually male) figured out who the leader really was, all that would change.

What I took to be scattershot thinking turned out to be Mother's way of playing the whole field. Although she was quite capable of going to the heart of an argument, she would rarely take the route of frontal assault. Rather, she would bounce ideas and comments all around the periphery until she had defined the field on which she wanted to play and given it a context to her liking. Only then would she start to draw the knot.

As a strategy, it was marvelous. Those who opposed her rarely knew where she was going until she got there, and then it was too late. Not only was the die cast by that time, but more often than not the opposition was thoroughly neutralized. Never opposing the other side directly gave Mother the space to effect alliances and isolate detractors. She knew all about not opposing force with force.

Above everything else, Mother was a lady. Not that she was just nice or proper—although she was certainly both of these—but rather, she gave deep meaning to the words *honor* and *respect*. No matter what side of an issue you might be on, and particularly if you were on the side opposite to her own, you were treated well. Doubtless I have idealized a most important person, and certainly I can recollect those times that Mother was less than perfect, even petty or manipulative. But through it all came a fundamental honor and respect that more than redeemed the nastier parts.

This aspect of Mother's strategy (and character) became obvious in a number of ways, but most particularly when she gave a small party. Crowds of people and the noisy party scene were not Mother's cup of tea. But for friends, and especially for colleagues when she wanted to get something done, a small gathering, informally but exquisitely architected, was the chosen field of play. No speeches, no dramatic appeals to recalcitrant opponents' "better nature," nor charismatic summoning of the troops—just infinite attention to the details of making guests feel comfortable, honored, and respected.

As a witness, and sometime butler, to such occasions, I confess to a certain mystification as to how it all worked. A quiet word here, a fresh drink there, gentle corralling of complementary conversationalists into an eddy of the party's flow—Mother didn't like to dance, but she surely knew how to effect the magical movement of genuine communication. Call it what you will, I can only call it leadership.

A son's remembrances of his mother can scarcely qualify as objective reporting; yet I have seen the patterns and approaches manifested by my mother practiced by other ladies of a certain age. Too old to be part of, and possibly comfortable with, the women's movement of recent years, and too young to have participated in the suffragette marches, they nonetheless evidenced a style and power of leadership from which I think we can learn much. On the outside of formal power, they held enormous power to effect the changes they held to be important. Their mode of operation was not the standard pattern. They gained power by giving it away, competed by cooperating, rarely if ever opposed force with force, played the whole field with an acute sense of the dance, and above all, honored and respected everybody, and most especially their opponents. In a day when confrontational, charismatic, directive leadership is often idolized in its absence, it may well be that its loss is not to be lamented. Useful alternatives are available.

CHAPTER 5

Life in the Underground

The Basics of Leadership

Although Mother and her friends might not have liked the image, I think they operated very much in the underground. From the viewpoint of those "in charge," they were definitely off the books and not in control of the normal levers of power. Despite this—actually, *because* of it—they managed to accomplish much deemed impossible by those who thought they determined the nature of possibility. Leadership in the underground was not without its power, albeit power that manifests itself in some basic, counterintuitive, not to say mysterious ways.

As we experience the dissolution of the structures and controls by which we have always done business, we may do well to take another look at that elemental world. The return to basics is partially a nostalgic revisitation of a simpler age, but it is not necessarily bad for that reason, because it may well be that we missed some important things along the way to our future.

On the simplest level, what we discover are the informal organization and the informal communication system. But these discoveries, I think, are only the beginning, and a rather superficial beginning at that. Under normal circumstances, the informal system is understood to be more primitive and less sophisticated and evolved than the formal system. There is a sense in which we have intentionally, and thankfully, left the informal way of doing business behind in our ascent to the present rational mode. The informal system is seen as "less," and the formal system as "more."

The history of organization, as indeed the history of the species, would seem to justify such a view. There was a time when all of us were hunters and gatherers, operating in a very loose and informal set of relationships. As we matured, however, we settled down to create villages and marketplaces. We got "organized."

Businesses follow a similar developmental pattern. Once upon a time in every business, the entrepreneur walked the land: primal, exciting, but basically disorganized. Then there came a day when rational management emerged to straighten out the mess. Steve Jobs was replaced by John Scully at Apple Computer, for example, and entrepreneurial zeal gave way to scientific management. The system was born. (Interestingly, Jobs has now replaced Scully, and we will see how the tale turns out.)

Each stage of organizational evolution[1] has its own style of leadership. The entrepreneurial leader is heavy on charisma, challenge, and pure, raw energy. The leader of rational business is heavy on structure, control, and logical decision making. Presumably the second style is an advance over the first, for after all, the system works—or so it seemed.

What happens when the system doesn't work? Obviously we fix the system. And when we run out of fixes, as we seem to be doing at the moment? Again the answer seems obvious: return to an earlier state. We all must become entrepreneurs again, or possibly *intrepreneurs,* to use the current jargon.[2]

But maybe, just maybe, our understanding of the entrepreneur and the entrepreneurial organization as a "lower" form of life was correct. Although the entrepreneur possesses many useful and exciting characteristics, such as innovation and high spirits, most of which seem sadly lacking in the increasingly drab world of the organizational system, it may also be true that you can never really go home again. After all, we have certainly had our entrepreneurs in recent days, but as romantic as the cowboys of the business world appear, in fact the days of the Wild West had their limitations. Are we then condemned to oscillate between the entrepreneur and the rational manager or leader, recognizing the insufficiencies of each but being unable to find anything new?

The problem, I suggest, is that we have been seeking salvation in terms of what we know, while refusing the more profitable, albeit dangerous, journey to the unknown, down to the true basics, into the underground. We are right in our assessment of the limitations of the entrepreneur. And unfortunately our emerging judgment about the rational manager, the leader who runs the system, is also correct. The future resides with neither. It lies deeper than that.

A true journey into the underground is not to be undertaken lightly, for once we are there we must confront a number of realities we would just as soon miss. It is not for nothing that we have attempted to construct a rational world in which the churning, chthonic forces lying beneath the surface of any human organization are controlled. Pure, raw human energy or spirit may be awesome and exciting, but it does tend to make a mess. We might start our journey with a story.

The Dragon's Tale

Once upon a time, back when the world was new, the Dragon lived in the deep. Known to the Israelites as T'hom and to the Babylonians as Tiamat, the Dragon was mother of all, a dark force whose dominion spread from shore to shore. In passion, her awesome power shaped and sculpted the land—a cliff of granite destroyed, a dazzling white beach created. Islands and lagoons, sand bars and channels emerged in response to her restless movement. But when she smiled, the seas rippled in delight. Dancing sunbeams made diamonds in the waves, and gentle swells, resonating to her pleasure, caressed the shores of a thousand lands, sending warm tides surging through quiet wetlands, the swampy nursery of all living things.

Then one day, by means now lost in the mists of time, the Dragon was lured from the sea and banished to a cave. For reasons that seemed good at the time, it was decided by the powers that were to put an end to the restless destruction and creation of the Dragon. Too many towns had found their waterfronts endangered, and islanders had grown tired of losing treasured beaches to the Dragon's playful sport. It was bad for business and bad for the tourists. So something had to be done, and off to the cave she went.

As things turned out, the sea is still roiled by the children of the Dragon, but the Dragon passes sunless days confined to the Stygian gloom. The ripples no longer mirror her smile, the swells do not resonate to her pleasure. Should despair and anger drive the Dragon to leave her gloomy abode, the way is blocked by a guard at the gate. St. George by name, this fabled knight stands watch with sharpened sword and stout spear, keeping the Dragon under control.

Once, it is said, the Dragon broke loose while St. George was off on a coffee break. In the twinkling of an eye the gates were passed and the violent passion, compressed in the cave, poured out across the land. The destruction was truly awesome. Whole villages disappeared in sheets of flame, and castles were tumbled into their moats. For days the Dragon raged, until St. George and a hastily assembled band of junior knights corralled the beast.

From that day until this, the Dragon has been contained. It is said that the earth trembles with her rage, but very few know the place she is held, and fewer still dare visit. Those who do visit stand far off, protected by the might of St. George, whispering tales of the day the Dragon broke free.

Quite recently, however, a strange, heretical thought has appeared in the land. What if the Dragon were not the terrible beast so horrendously described in song and fable? Angry for sure, but wouldn't you be angry if you had been locked in a cave for millennia? Perhaps the Dragon is only lonely? What would it mean to make friends with the Dragon?

Leadership: Making Friends with the Dragon

In forms almost too numerous to count, the Dragon has appeared as a common element in the imagination and mythology of humankind. The way the Dragon has been treated, however, differs widely around the world. In the West (including the ancient Near East from which much of the Western tradition has emerged), the Dragon is an awesome beast, as in the tale just told. Fear is the common response to the Dragon, and much knightly valor has been dedicated to keeping the beast at bay and under control.

In the Far East, on the other hand, reaction to the Dragon is strikingly different, although the basic image remains remarkably the same. In China and Japan, the Dragon is also an awesome beast, surrounded by smoke and fire and inhabiting the underground. But reaction to the Dragon is the exact opposite of the West's controlling approach. One must learn to respect the Dragon and learn to live with it. In lighter moments, for example, during the New Year's celebration, people will dance with the Dragon. And in truth, nothing of import can go on until the Dragon dances.

The Dragon, in all of its manifestations, points to the world of deep, primal power, the surging world of Spirit from which everything, so goes the story, emerges. In the West the effort is to control, to channel, to render harmless. In the East the effort is toward alignment, seeking to intuit the flow and move with it. For the West, life with the Dragon represents struggle and conflict. And the hero—may we say leader—is the one who does both best. In the East, life with the Dragon is, ideally, harmonious, and the leader is the one who shows the way.

Who knows whether Dragons exist? In a very real sense, it doesn't make any difference, for it is certain that Dragons existed, and continue to exist, in our minds' images. To the extent that the pictures we hold in our minds tell us something useful about who we are, and about who we might become, our Western perception of the Dragon suggests that we are very uncomfortable with deep, surging forces that lie beyond our control.

That insight, if such it be, might best be left on the analyst's couch, except for the fact that there apparently are a number of Dragons loose in our world at the moment, none of which we seem likely to control. Might it not be that there is some wisdom available from the East? Would it not be well to make friends with the Dragon?

The Yin and Yang of Leadership

Making friends with the Dragon is not to be undertaken lightly, nor should it be confused with what we might call "becoming good buddies." The powers represented by the Dragon are real, awesome, and truly beyond our control. Those who presume to assert control, in the sense in which we in the West commonly mean, will discover that the Dragon simply either hides out or explodes. Neither result is useful. By the same token, efforts to trivialize (to be good buddies) are productive of nasty surprises. Precisely when we think we have it all together, things get out of hand. Making friends with the Dragon requires a strong sense of *balance* and *appropriateness,* which is where the notion of yin and yang becomes useful.

The Eastern notion of yin and yang describes the conditions under which friendship may be developed and leadership may be exercised. In the case of friendship, yin and yang are the *balance of opposites:* masculine and feminine, light and dark, order and disorder, chaos and cosmos. They are inherently paradoxical, and many of us in the West do not like paradoxes. Indeed, when we confront such things, something in our mental apparatus says "contradiction." From there we proceed to decide which element of the paradox is "wrong." Our rule of thumb is either/or—either male or female, light or dark, order or disorder.

Much of the rest of the world looks at the same information and concludes both/and." It is always a question of balance. More than balance, it is *necessary* polarity. The light illuminates only in the darkness, order becomes manifest only out of disorder, female assumes meaning only in relationship to male, and vice versa in all cases. There is no right or wrong, better or worse. Always there is both/and.

For leadership, the polarities of yin and yang represent the range of opportunity, the definition of the field on which leadership will be exercised. It is a large field and a broad range. Anything less will restrict the opportunities for growth. Thus, when the world is seen only in masculine terms, the feminine aspects of warmth, nurture, acceptance, caring, and support tend to disappear. But if the situation were reversed, so that only the feminine was apparent, the necessary masculine elements of challenge, thrust, judgment, and distinction would be lost. Challenge left unbalanced by caring is destructive, but acceptance without critical judgment is mush.

What is true for the polarities of male and female is equally true for order and disorder. Leadership that perceives order (cosmos) as its mission, and disorder (chaos) as the enemy will totally miss the opportunities present when the established forms and structures fall away, allowing for the creation of new and more appropriate ones. Such leadership will spend its time holding on to what *was* (order), instead of nurturing the growing edge appearing in chaos. There is no question that chaos is a mess, but messes, like swamps, turn out to be the nutrient seedbed of emergent life.

Our Western inability to hold the polarities and accept the paradox of yin and yang has led to extremes of leadership style that at best are amusing and at worst are horribly destructive. When leadership operates exclusively in the masculine aspect, the single "powerful one" takes charge from the top. Decisions are made, but few care to follow because there is no ownership. When leadership swings to the opposite side and the feminine dominates, "participative management" discusses, and discusses, and discusses. Everybody owns it, but nobody does anything. There is a time for talk and there is a time to walk. The question is, when and what is *appropriate?*

A sense of appropriateness is critical, but it is also maddeningly elusive. As in poker, you have to know when to hold and know when to fold.[3] Should you ask, "When is that?" the usual answer comes back to haunt you: you just have to know—all of which tells us that appropriateness is not a matter of formula. Three parts participation to one part decision may look good on the printed page, but it (or any other formulation) simply does not work.

What cannot be achieved by formula may be achieved by attention to the flow of Spirit, and by continued practice. Just as a champion poker player does not emerge from a single session at the table, and certainly not from a quick reading of the rule book, so in the domain of the Dragon: effective leadership simply does not happen without practice. When the field is known, however, and the cues are recognized by a practiced eye, amazing things can, and do, happen. Spirit will be focused and empowered to get the job done, whatever that job might be. And creating the time and space for Spirit to show up is what leadership is all about.

NOTES

1. Private communication.
2. The term *intrepreneur* is the invention of Gifford Pinchot, and refers to entrepreneurs who work inside a company.
3. For nonpoker players, it may be useful to know that a central part of the game is bluffing (fooling) your opponents into

thinking that you hold better cards than you actually do. If the bluff is successful, the opponents will lay down their cards (fold) in surrender—at which point you win the game. If you get caught, however, (that is, if somebody "calls your bluff"), the tables will be turned. Ergo, you've got to know when to hold and know when to fold.

CHAPTER 6

Spirit and Leadership

For many in the West, Spirit is nothing.[1] Operating under the premise that if you can't count it, it doesn't exist, the conclusion is that Spirit is not there, or if it is there, it can't amount to much. At the level of proof there is little if anything that can be done to alter this position, for having started with the premise of "countability," the conclusion is inescapable. Yet despite the obvious inescapability of the logic, there appears to be a growing sense that this logic need not be the only one used.

Perhaps it is only the uneasiness of the times but conversations about Spirit now seem to appear in some of the strangest places. As long ago as 1987, for example, a major corporation took out a full-page ad to proclaim that a central corporate goal is to "sustain the Spirit."[2] Perhaps they didn't mean it, but it is interesting that they felt free enough to say something like that. And of course there has been a recent outbreak of spirituality in business, a phenomenon that leaves me a little uncomfortable. It tends to be off-putting to many; but most worrisome, I think, is that it may trivialize the subject. In present discourse, spirituality often shows up as an add-on—we have business to which we may add a spiritual dimension. For me there is no question of adding on—everything begins with Spirit, which shows up (for better or worse) as the business we do. Spirituality does have a place, but not as a special department in the organization, the Department of Spirituality, managed of course by the director of spirituality. Spirituality is what we all do twenty-four hours a day as we acknowledge our existence as Spirit and learn to live with that reality.

Of course there have always been words about Spirit in common conversation, as in *team spirit, esprit de corps,* and the like. But now, somehow, the concept of Spirit seems rather more important. A senior executive in the midst of a very nasty take-over battle was overheard to say, "It is remarkable that when everything else is falling apart, we still have our spirit. If we lose that, I think we have lost everything." I believe he was right. When Spirit disappears, there is not much left.

I take it as a given that Spirit is the most critical element of any organization. With Spirit of the appropriate quantity, quality, and direction, almost anything is possible. Without Spirit, the simplest task becomes a monumental obstacle. Furthermore, it is in the domain of Spirit that leadership operates. Though it may be true that leaders have a multitude of very practical tasks, they have one task that outweighs all others: to care for Spirit.

Linking leadership and Spirit presents few problems at the level of casual conversation. Even the popular press has good words to say about "inspiring leadership"—and *inspiration,* after all, means "to fill with Spirit." Quarterbacks inspire their teams, generals inspire their troops, and presidents are supposed to inspire their companies and countries. That leadership, inspiration, and Spirit all go together seems like a no-news item.

The problem is not making the connection but, rather, what to do after that. And here again it appears that the possibility of making a useful, novel statement is limited. University libraries and executive bookshelves are filled to overflowing with innumerable tomes on the subject, ranging from deep studies to shallow nostrums detailing the "Seven Easy Steps to Inspired Leadership." Yet something is missing, either in the literature, in its reception, or both.

I think that what is missing is a profound sense of the depth of the matter. Leadership is often spoken of as if it were simply advanced management. The presumption is that whatever the manager is supposed to do, the leader does more of and better. Leadership is not advanced management; in fact, it is radically different from management, and to equate or confuse the two is to miss an essential distinction, and that distinction, if observed, can take us to the heart of the matter.

Before going further, I need to make it exquisitely clear that I am not juxtaposing managers and leaders; rather, I am concerned with functions or roles. The truth of the matter is that we all lead and we all manage.

In general, we are quite clear about what managers are supposed to do. They control the system, whatever that system might be. And the operative word is *control*. A good manager makes the plan, manages to the plan, and meets the plan. The details are taken care of, the aberrancies are controlled, and the problems are solved.

It has almost become popular to denigrate managers, as if they were somehow a lesser breed, and not all that useful. Nothing could be further from the truth. For as long as we have systems that are basically workable in the extant environment, we need managers—very good managers.

In the post–World War II years, the manager reigned supreme. Everyone wanted to be a manager, and management, quite rightly, was understood to reside at the top of the heap. Under relatively stable conditions, or conditions in which things change in a linearly predictable fashion, the role of management is primary. But when the balance swings to nonstability and change occurs in radical, discontinuous jumps, the skills of management don't work quite as well as they used to.

The tasks of management and leadership are, I believe, separate and distinct. To manage is to control; to lead is to liberate. To manage is to work at the level of the system; to lead is to work in the depths beneath the system, in the primal areas where the Dragon lives.

Leadership Is Liberation: Being out of Control, and Loving It

In the everyday world, we take it as a given that when we lose control we are crazy, and indeed there is no small amount of experimental evidence that people with little or no perceived control over their lives are driven crazy.

Craziness, in the domain of Spirit, is the perception that *we are in control*. The reality is that Spirit moves as it wants, changing shape, form, intensity, and direction with the speed of a whim and the passage of a mood. Just when you think you've got it, like a wisp of smoke it passes through your hands to appear in another place, or disappears all together.

Talk like this may seem imprecise, as indeed it is, but the experience alluded to is familiar to everyone. The coach of an outstanding team knows all to well that having the best players, game plan, and coaching staff does not automatically secure the championship. "Some days the guys are hot, and some days they're not." Corporate executives know that although state-of-the-art plant and facilities, matched with skilled workers and managers, are strong cards to hold, the competitive edge is not guaranteed.

At the other extreme are those instances where few of the accoutrements of success are in hand, and yet miraculously—or at least it appears to be a miracle—good things happen. In the nick of time, despite all odds, at the last moment, the deal is closed, the game is won, the company is saved. In retrospect, it is always nice to feel that everything was part of the plan. But those who were there, and particularly those who assumed the role of leadership, know differently. If it was a plan, it was surely a different kind of plan, for things turned out as nobody had any right or reason to expect. In private moments of honesty, it is often reported that things began to work precisely when all attempts at making them work were given up. Being in control, paradoxically, meant being out of control and going with it. But being out of control does not mean being without principle.

The Four Immutable Principles of Spirit

Spirit plays by its own principles, which from the viewpoint of standard management practice are not only strange but also aggravating in the extreme. I am not sure, of course, that these principles are immutable, but they always seem to apply. They are as follows:

1. Whoever comes is the right people.
2. Whatever happens is the only thing that could have happened.
3. Whenever it starts is the right time.
4. When it's over, it's over.

The Four Immutable Principles occurred to me originally as a rather facetious way to describe the operative conditions in meetings and conferences, and particularly in that special sort of conference now known as Open Space. I then discovered that these principles were no joke, and further, that violating them inevitably produced disastrous results. I admit that it seems as though the principles suggest a total "just let it happen" approach, prescriptive of failure. To be sure, one must make one's best effort to get ready. Details of time and space must be attended to. But when all that is done, or done as well as can be expected, then the only thing to do is follow the principles. Like it or not, whoever comes is not only the right people, they are the only ones there, and

> **THE FOUR IMMUTABLE PRINCIPLES OF SPIRIT**
>
> *Whoever comes is the right people.*
>
> *Whatever happens is the only thing that could have happened.*
>
> *Whenever it starts is the right time.*
>
> *When it's over, it's over.*

whatever happens is going to happen with them, or not at all. Recognizing these principles saves untold amounts of anxiety and "might have beens," which can become so overpowering that the real, present opportunities are overlooked. The Four Immutable Principles work, I believe, in meetings and conferences because they are descriptive of the way Spirit works.

First Principle: Whoever comes is the right people. This principle reminds us that Spirit cannot be forced. In situations in which word has come down from on high that a certain position or initiative is an organizational "must" that requires "spirited participation," there is absolutely no way in the world to ensure that all members of the organization will buy in. Seeking such a result not only guarantees failure, but it is also the total perversion of what Spirit is all about. Spirit forced is Spirit killed.

The fact that some people do not feel inclined to join is not an indication of failure, unless it is defined as such. If, however, the would-be leader observes the First Principle, there is a high likelihood that not only will Spirit rise, but it will also be infinitely deeper and richer than could ever have been imagined. All who choose to participate will do so from, and for, their passion. Such passion provides the essential, powerful source of innovation and performance.

Second Principle: Whatever happens is the only thing that could have happened. This principle reminds us that leadership is not control. Control is management. Leadership is, rather, the creation of a nurturant open space in which genuine human fulfillment may be achieved. The problem is that would-be leaders, for their own reasons of insecurity, often feel they must manage. After all, things could get out of control. The truth of the matter is, not only can things get out of control but it is virtually guaranteed if Spirit is really up and powerful.

This is a difficult point for one who leads. There is an understandable feeling that, having accepted the responsibility of leadership, the leader must also specify exactly how everything will turn out. The understandability of this feeling does not change its negative impact. As all parents come to appreciate, although giving birth to a child creates some proprietary interests, it is not license to specify outcome. To forget this is to invite rebellion or withdrawal. The same is true with Spirit.

Third Principle: Whenever it starts is the right time. In a curious and important way, Spirit exists outside of time. Indeed, Spirit creates time. For Westerners driven by the clock, this is difficult to deal with, but the rest of the world understands that truly important events always make their own time. Actually, we in the West understand this, too. We say, without thinking about it, that the current year is A.D. 1998. We tend to overlook that this dating method has meaning only in the context of a particular manifestation of Spirit: the birth of Jesus of Nazareth, which occurred 1,998 years ago. No matter what we as individuals may think about that particular person, there is no question that even the Western time system is Spirit based. Of course, if Spirit manifested in a different person or place, a different dating system is used. Thus the Jews are a millennium or so ahead of the Christians, and for the Hindus, the birth of Vishnu some 4,000 years ago is central.

When Spirit appears, it doesn't happen according to the calendar. Whenever it happens is not only the right time, but it's also its own time. Needless to say, senior executives hoping to raise the Spirit of a place find this principle annoying, but that doesn't change its power. The emergence of Spirit will inevitably frustrate the keepers of the corporate calendar.

Fourth Principle: When it's over, it's over. The manifestation of Spirit as all things appearing in time and space has a lifespan, and when it's over, it's over. Certainly Spirit may be renewed, but there comes a time when a particular form simply runs out of steam.

The central task of leadership is to liberate and focus Spirit, guided by the Four Immutable Principles. In practice, however, there are some more specific functions of leadership, which we will examine here and in the following chapters. The five functions of leadership are (1) to evoke Spirit with vision, (2) to grow Spirit with collective storytelling, (3) to sustain Spirit with structure, (4) to comfort Spirit at the end, and (5) to raise Spirit, thereby enabling the conditions of renewal.

THE FIVE FUNCTIONS OF LEADERSHIP

1. *To evoke Spirit with vision.*

2. *To grow Spirit with collective storytelling.*

3. *To sustain Spirit with structure.*

4. *To comfort Spirit at the end.*

5. *To revive Spirit when grief works.*

NOTES

1. For example, Edgar Schein, writing in *Organizational Culture and Leadership* (San Francisco: Jossey-Bass, 1985), dispatches the whole notion of Spirit with a parenthetical phrase. He says, "In many cultures, what we would regard as the 'Spirit world,' *which is not real to us,* would be regarded as extremely real" (italics added). My point is not to pick on Schein but rather to agree with him. In the West, the notion of Spirit typically elicits the sort of treatment Schein gives it.
2. The corporation was Shell Canada, and the publication was the program for the Winter Olympics in Calgary, Ontario, 1987.

CHAPTER 7

The First Function of Leadership

Evoking Spirit with Vision

Leadership is not a matter of command and control. It is the evocation and alignment of Spirit. Spirit cannot be commanded, but it may be invited. Spirit cannot be coerced, but it may be channeled. Spirit rarely, if ever, responds to answers; rather, it responds to questions, which create the nurturant Open Space in which it may flow. Vision poses the question that creates the space into which Spirit flows and becomes powerful.

It has become popular for organizations to engage in "visioning," the end product of which is a vision statement. The advent of visioning as a legitimate corporate practice is certainly to be applauded, for it recognizes precisely the realities we are discussing. But the equation of vision with a vision statement is at best weak, and at worst a total perversion of what vision is all about.

There is an acid test for the effectiveness of vision statements. One simply posts them on the wall and asks the group involved, Would you be willing to give your life for that? Admittedly this may sound rather extreme, but we typically spend more time "on the job" than doing anything else, with the possible exception of sleeping. If the answer is no, there is reasonable indication that the statement is only words, untouched by the power of vision.

Upon examination, it usually turns out that such ineffective vision statements emerge in one of two ways. Usually they are the product of the titular leader's description of what the business is all about, issued very much in the style of a policy directive. Alternatively, the vision statement comes into being after endless hours of committee meetings. This is simply a case of the right idea addressed in the wrong way, for vision is not a policy statement, or the product of a committee. It comes from an entirely different place.

The Genesis of Vision

Vision emerges from the depths. It comes from the domain of the Dragon (see Chapter Five), in ways that contravene logical policy-making or standard committee procedure. The exact mechanics are a matter of currently evolving discovery, but they seem to have a lot to do with the powers of intuition and the operation of what now would be called the "right brain."[1] But if the precise mechanics are less than clear, the phenomenon has long been known.

The birthing place of vision is the Open Space created when things fall apart and difference is perceived. It emerges when an old way of being or of doing things is no longer appropriate or effective and a new way has yet to emerge. The instigating moment may be the end of a particular business or product, or the exhaustion of a theoretical concept or way of looking at things. In extremes it may be the dissolution of a social order. In all cases the instigating factor is the awareness of ending.

This moment is far from comfortable, for by definition all the usual supportive elements defining the way things are supposed to happen cease to exist. Even the stouthearted will experience fear and a sense of emptiness. But emptiness is the clearing in the forest of everyday activities, the Open Space in which vision may emerge.

The good news of Open Space at the point of ending is that things can be seen with a degree of clarity that the business of everyday life obscures. When all the schedules, to-do lists, and committee meetings are over, there arrives a profound and rich moment in which it is possible to ask what it all means anyhow. Attempts to fill the Open Space with yesterday's answers are automatic, but futile.

At its point of genesis, vision appears in forms most notable for their variety. For some people it is a "still small voice." Einstein apparently *heard* his visions as music, which he later translated into mathematics. My cottonwood tree experience was purely visual. I could "see" the connection of all beings with the intensity of a waking dream. Others report experiencing various colors, shapes, and sounds, made significant only by the inescapable awareness that meaning, unclear and undefined to be sure, was present.

I use the word *inescapable* with intention. Vision is compelling, even compulsive, which is both the problem and the power. Recurrent images (in whatever format) tend to be crazy-making, and those who report such recurrent images are often taken to be crazy. Indeed, the difference between hallucination and emergent vision may be almost imperceptible. The power of vision also derives from this sense of inescapability and compulsion. Visionaries typically are driven people. In the vernacular, they see things that others don't see, march to a different drummer, play by new rules. They tend to be strange and difficult to get along with. Their strangeness or differentness is easy to understand, for by definition they have perceived, in the Open Space, some difference that makes a difference, to them. Where others see only ending (destruction) or nothing at all, those possessed by a vision see some difference, small or large, that renders the future a possibility, and marks the first step toward a new version of reality.

If visionaries are compulsive, they are also frustrating, for they tend to talk in repetitive circles, struggling to bring their object of awareness into focus. Their compulsion gives them the appearance of certainty. Their lack of clarity often makes them an object of scorn. It is very difficult to be convinced of something that nobody else can see, and it is just as hard to live with one who suffers from such a conviction. But all of that comes with the territory.

It is more than a little tempting to question a source of a vision. Strict behaviorists, convinced that human behavior in all its forms is simply the outcome of electrochemical reactions, will posit a bad dinner the night before. Neurophysiologists might propose the right brain. Humanistic psychologists offer the unconscious mind. And mystics will identify the great cosmic abyss. I don't know, but if pressed I would suggest that vision comes from the domain of the Dragon, that it is a manifestation of Spirit. Although the question is important, the answer, for our purposes, is not essential. It is only important that vision begins in Open Space with the perception of difference.

Sharing Vision: From One to the Many

Vision, for all its power and potential, is not worth a great deal as long as it remains the private preserve of a single individual. Once shared, however, it has the capacity to focus and galvanize Spirit in remarkable and often breathtaking ways. The distance, however, from the one to the many is not small, and traversing that distance cannot be done without cost.

One of the best descriptions of the passage of an emergent vision is provided by Thomas Kuhn in his book *The Structure of Scientific Revolutions.*[2] Although Kuhn might not like the suggestion that he is writing about vision, I believe that to be the case. His actual subject matter is the arrival of the different scientific conceptual models, or in his terms, *paradigms,* through which the world is understood.

Stripped to essentials, a paradigm is a way of looking at reality that makes sense; it arises from the end of an older version, with some significant difference perceived. Although vision may lack some of the scientific precision possessed by paradigm, I take them to be the same.

We learn from Kuhn that the progress of scientific knowledge does not occur in the nice linear pattern that high school science classes sometimes suggest. It occurs in great, tumultuous leaps, when an older vision proves inadequate. The story is that once upon a time there was a standard way of looking at the world (be it Ptolemaic, Babylonian, Copernican, or Newtonian) that worked quite well, until it was noticed that everything didn't quite fit in. So the theory was adjusted to fit the anomalies. Its proponents said something like, "The theory is true, except for. . . ." After a while the exceptions grew greater than the rule, and something had to give. But not without a struggle.

Those who lived by the old world view were loath to change. Things were quite comfortable as they saw it, and dealing with reality in a new way was not quite what they had in mind. At the same time, a small, growing band found the exceptions inescapable and the rule intolerable, so they imagined (may we say visioned?) a different way of looking at things.

Heresy! Quite literally. People paid in blood, and often with their lives, for seeing things differently. And those on the "other side" resisted the change, quite understandably. For implicit in the acceptance of change was the acknowledgment of the passage of the old order. Those who had defined their lives in terms of the old order discovered that their lives were not only different but also finished. Not pleasant.

Gathering Spirit: Qualities of Effective Visions

Before vision can focus Spirit, it must first gather Spirit, and that is no simple task, especially when the folks involved are not at all sure that the new direction is in their best interest, or that they want to be "gathered." All of which leads to some suggestions on the specifications of effective vision—effective in the sense that it really inspires, or *inspirits*.

Powerful, effective visions have three qualities. They are big, attractive, and doable. *Big* is not a matter of being grandiose, but rather, of being commodious. The vision must be big enough to actually gather all the Spirit inside. Obviously, spatial talk is not really appropriate when speaking of Spirit, but it may get the idea across. The point is that the vision must be large enough to provide room for all the folks who are likely to participate, and more. There must be space for all essential points of view, frames of reference, skills, occupations, and whatever. When vision is too small it is exclusive, and the power of vision to gather Spirit will be vitiated from the start, no matter how good or exciting the vision may be.

Not only must vision be big enough for all the players as they are at the moment, but there must also be plenty of room to grow. *Vision is never an answer but always a question that initiates a quest toward the fulfillment of the participants.* It is a journey that elicits the best that everybody has, and simultaneously provides the space in which they might become infinitely more than they ever imagined. Certainly a vision must have a focus, just as a journey must have a destination, but when the journey's end is totally known in advance, it is scarcely a worthwhile undertaking.

Mystery and awe are experienced in the presence of powerful visions, which also usually means the presence of fear. In extremes, fear may prevent some people from entering into the vision, and it may well be that they should not go on the journey. But unless the tingle of fear is known somewhere at the beginning, there is a strong likelihood, indeed an absolute certainty, that the vision is too small. Tame visions go nowhere.

The second characteristic of a powerful, effective vision is *attractiveness*. Spirit cannot be coerced; it must always be invited, and few will accept an unattractive invitation. If vision provides the space for growth, it must also propose an appealing direction for growth. Nobody has to enter into the vision. The test for the individual is always, Do I want to be like that?

Finally, a powerful, effective vision must be *doable*. Doable has two senses. First, it should be technically feasible. Lots of big, attractive visions have foundered for the simple reason that there was no way on earth they could be accomplished. Obviously, good visions will, and must, push the limits of technology, but if there is no sense of a likely, positive outcome, the possibility of eliciting a reasonable number of "cojourneyers" is limited at best.

The second sense of doable is "historically possible." Many visions that are big, attractive, and technically feasible are just inappropriate to the circumstances of those addressed. The feeling here is, That might be somebody else's vision, but not ours.

A very good example of historical nondoability appears in the reaction of non-Western countries to the vision of Western economic development. Few citizens of non-Western countries who are knowledgeable about the Western vision would deny either its bigness or its attractiveness, and its technical feasibility has been amply demonstrated. But there remains a real sense that, good though it may be, it is not them. Westerners, of course, have viewed this reaction as being something between madness and idiocy, but it may well turn out that the doubters were right not only in terms of their own history but also in terms of the history (nature) of the planet. Western technology, as a driving vision, clearly has its limitations, as evidenced by its propensity for fouling the nest in which we all live.

Vision and the Four Immutable Principles

One might suspect that having these three criteria for effective vision firmly in hand, it should now be possible to design an irresistible vision. I think that is unlikely, for the simple reason that

Spirit doesn't work that way. It is true that Spirit seems to follow certain principles, but they are not mechanistically coercive. More accurately, to the extent that there are mechanics they are the mechanics of the quantum and not of Newton.

Newton tells us that, when dealing with such things as a large rock, given a lever of sufficient length and strength, combined with some leverage point, the rock *will* move. Quantum mechanics tells a different story. In the world of high energy, the principle of indeterminacy applies. Although it may sound rather odd, this principle says that given enough rocks, levers, and time, some rock, somewhere, will probably move. In other words, with thorough study and careful work, one may raise probability, but never to the level of certainty. Raising probability with vision and Spirit requires that we remember the Four Immutable Principles introduced in the previous chapter:

The first principle, *Whoever comes is the right people*, reminds us that becoming inspired, electrified, and turned on by any vision is always a matter of personal choice. A vision forced is a vision killed. Vision, after all, is a question and an invitation to fulfillment.

The second principle, *Whatever happens is the only thing that could have happened*, reminds us that visions, like parents, that specify end results in detail are bound to be frustrated. Such visions become limitations and not evocations. Be prepared to be surprised.

The third principle, *Whenever it starts is the right time*, reminds us that vision does not occur in time; rather, time occurs in the context of vision. When vision strikes, it creates its own time, and that is one of the ways in which we know it was real vision and not just a flash in the pan.

The fourth principle, *When it's over, it's over*, reminds us that visions have a life span, and when it is over, it is over. Certainly visions may be renewed or sustained, but there comes a time when a particular vision simply runs out of steam, and its capacity to focus Spirit wanes and ceases. That is true in the record of scientific visions: the Ptolemaic picture of the universe gave way to Copernicus, from thence to Newton, and on to the quantum theorists. Each of these visions, in its own time, created a frame of reference from which to make sense of what was going on in the world. Then the exceptions appeared and the anomalies grew. It was not that the vision was no longer true; it simply lacked the power to focus Spirit. When it's over, it's over.

NOTES

1. The literature in this area grows geometrically by the year, but for some general reading, consult Willis W. Harman and Howard Rheingold, *Higher Creativity: Liberating the Unconscious for Breakthrough Insights* (Los Angeles: Tarcher, 1984) and Philip Goldberg, *The Intuitive Edge: Understanding and Developing Intuition* (Los Angeles: Tarcher, 1983).
2. Thomas Kuhn, *The Structure of Scientific Revolutions* (Chicago: University of Chicago Press, 1962).

The Second Function of Leadership

Growing Spirit Through Collective Storytelling

Spirit evoked by vision can begin to realize its potential not only when the vision is shared but also when it is grown. Leadership has a central part to play in this process through collective storytelling.

Storytelling may seem a rather weak reed with which to build an organization, but that is to misunderstand the power of stories. When I say *story*, I am referring not to some idle or amusing tale, but rather, to the central vehicle through which the Spirit of an organization is gathered and focused on the job at hand. The story is the *organizational mythology.*

Having said "mythology," I may have made the situation even less comprehensible, for to many people myth is not merely an idle tale, but it is by definition *untrue.* Contrary to this view, myth is neither true nor untrue. Rather, it is *behind* or *beneath* truth; it establishes the context within which people talk to one another and determine the truth. A short example may clarify.

What's the Story Anyhow? The Power of Myth

Suppose you walk into a business as a prospective employee. You are presumably interested in all the normal, first-line questions about compensation, benefits, job description, hours of operation, and organizational structure, the answers to which are provided to you through a series of tables, charts, and manuals. Necessary as that material is, it seems a little dry and abstract. You press deeper, to questions that are more amorphous but very important: questions about working conditions—what it would feel like to work in this place, and what it all really means. Some answers will appear just by walking around and looking at the physical circumstances, the layout of the facility, the color on the walls, the patterns of activity; but sooner or later you will find it necessary to identify some kind of context in order to determine what is different about this place compared to all others. And most important, do you really want to be a part of it?

At such a moment it is almost guaranteed that you will search out an individual with whom you feel comfortable and ask, What's the story anyhow? What's *really* going on? Questions such as these are best asked after hours, in a bar, a coffee shop, or over dinner—all places far removed from the official presentations. This is the time to get down to where the "rubber meets the road," to the nitty-gritty, to hear the "real story."

If you then reflect on what you have learned, you may be surprised to find that the real story has very little to do with the cold, objective facts, which you probably already knew. The real story ends up being closer to war stories.

In a curious way, the facts of the matter don't make any difference; indeed, you may have a strong suspicion that the events recounted never happened at all. Regardless, something important is being communicated through what seem to be incidental examples. That something is the feeling or meaning of a place, which establishes the context within which all of the bits and pieces of an organization's life start to make sense. Without stretching the point, we might even say that the stories tell us something about the Spirit of a place. In fact, these stories do more than that; they actually bring us into immediate encounter with that strange thing we call Spirit.

Suppose that in our imaginary conversation over a cup of coffee the tale goes like this:

> I don't know what they told you up in the front office, but let me tell you like it really is. Last week, the boss called in five managers, looked at the numbers, and fired the bottom two managers. No warning, no separation packages, just *out.* I've got to tell you, this is a schlock outfit. Top management is just out for itself.

No graduate degree in organizational psychology is needed to assess the quality of Spirit in this place. And the fact that there may have been six managers instead of five, and that only one got fired and not two, makes very little difference in the assessment. The story very quickly communicates the reality of Spirit in the place, and it is significant not only in itself but also in the fact that your confidant chose to tell it to you. Even if the events described never happened, the very telling of the story gives you a fast picture of what is going on.

Now, obviously one story once told does not a myth make. So the next day you go back and casually ask a number of people if they ever heard "the one about," and although the details and numbers vary widely, it becomes obvious that the story is there. Of course you may ask whether it is true, but probably by that point it becomes clear that the historical truth or falsehood of the tale is infinitely less important than the fact that it is being told.

Senior management, if confronted with the story, would undoubtedly be upset. Either they would try to downplay it by saying something like, "Aw, that's just a war story," or to discredit it by giving their version of the "facts." Neither approach is likely to be very effective, for to see the tale as just a war story is to overlook the intensity, even passion, with which it was told.

And giving management the facts will probably do little more than elicit a response like, "Well, that's their story."

The point is that *stories are powerful,* and they quickly and accurately reflect the Spirit of a place. Indeed, stories may be the most powerful element of organizational life, for they create the context within which everything that happens is interpreted. Saying that they are of no value, or that they are untrue, does not change their impact, as would quickly become clear were senior management to challenge this power. Should an official denial be issued, it would be taken as one more example of the duplicity of the top brass.

Even apparently positive efforts to change the story are likely to backfire. Imagine the general reaction if the fired managers were suddenly rewarded with a large separation package; there would be a lot of head scratching and wonderment about what "those SOBs are up to now, 'cause the story is. . . ."

The story is, and the story rules, which is why those who would lead must pay special attention to the tales that are told, or that could be told. For the story not only reflects the Spirit of a place, it shapes that Spirit and determines the ways it will behave.

Creating the Collective Story

The driving story of an organization is never just the story of the founder. It starts there, however, for vision is the organizational mythology in future tense. The power and the passion of the primary vision will be sufficient to generate excitement if that vision is big and attractive. And the excitement will be grounded and focused if, and as, the visionary begins to deal with doability, both technical and historical. A reasonable case must be made that the particular vision could be accomplished by those who hear the tale. But the essential shift from excited interest to committed involvement will take place only when the story becomes a collective one—no longer the founder's tale, but *our* story.

Captured imagination is the beginning, but its growth is essential. Inspiring a group of folks to believe in a new idea is always the first step, but letting that idea truly be theirs, to evolve as they are able and interested, marks the difference between short-term excitement and long-term commitment. From here on out the telling of the tale, even in the future tense, must be a collective activity, and it is exactly here that difficulty emerges. Visionaries, who have passionately given birth to new ideas, often find it difficult to let them go. And letting go is the essence of the operation.

It is an old truism that everybody sees everything from their own perspective, which means that when it comes to storytelling, each person must tell the story in his or her own way. Thus the marketer's story about the new product will probably have much more to say about the market than about the product, while the engineer will tell a tale with the opposite points of emphasis—and so it will go with all the potential participants. The opportunity for misunderstanding, because of differences in language, is acute, but the possibility that offense may be taken by the original visionary is higher.

As the story is told and retold from the several points of view, it will inevitably lose some of its original purity and focus, even as it gains breadth and depth. For the one who conceived the vision, this can be very painful indeed. Leadership here involves resisting offense and maintaining both the Open Space in which the story can be told and the focus of the tale, so it makes some sense. In a word, the Second Immutable Principle must be honored. No matter what the level of effort, it will remain true that whatever happens is the only thing that could have happened. Really letting go is essential.

Maintaining Open Space is a job that many will find difficult, for it involves *less* rather than *more*, waiting as opposed to moving. It is so tempting to fill up all the space with meetings and agendas, under the impression that something must be done. But this is to forget that the most fertile ground for the growth of Spirit is a question. The press of business and the passion of the visionary both drive for closure, but if those drives are heeded before all needed participants have an opportunity to contribute, the vision will die stillborn.

In practical detail, the leader must set the direction and manage the boundaries, while leaving almost everything else to the participants themselves. The leader's sole contributions may be only a few remarks to the effect that "I think we are in widgets and not whatsits."

The leader also has some work to do inside the boundaries, but that is not so much telling people what to do and think (outlining the plan) as it is making the connections and drawing out the implications of the several stories as they are told. It is a given that engineers and marketers, for example, will not understand each other at significant points. Even when they use the same words, they will be used with different meaning. Part of maintaining Open Space is constantly to clear away the obfuscation of jargon. There is no easy way to do this, for every professional group develops its own jargon and, worse than that, presumes that its language makes sense. One almost surefire way of reducing jargon is to invite people back to the level of storytelling, to move them away from abstractions and on to a narration of what "it" would look like if everything worked.

Leadership in Action

A story about leadership in action will make all of this more concrete. Several years ago, Owens/Corning Fiberglas (OCF) of Toledo, Ohio, had an unfortunate run-in with a small lumber yard on the West Coast by the name of Wicks. At the time, OCF was the dominant force in the fiberglass business. They invented the stuff and were making about four billion dollars worth of business each year. Known as Big Pink in the trade (pink for the color of their product, named in honor of their mascot, the Pink Panther), they set the trends and seemed secure in their position.

Then the sky fell. Wicks made a hostile run on Big Pink, and when the dust settled, management was still in control but under very reduced circumstances. To pay off the raiders and stock-holders, to say nothing of the army of lawyers and accountants, OCF went from having half a billion dollars in the bank to being a billion and a half in the hole—not a happy time. Businesses were sold, employees were terminated, and annual sales moved from four billion to a little over two billion dollars.

The hero of the moment was Max Weber, better known as Max, or Super Max. If you hear the stories, Max did everything. He sold the banks on a bailout package, sold businesses to make the terms, and led the troops to safety at enormous cost. Four-teen-hour days, seven-day weeks were the norm for all those who remained. After six months of this behavior, there was good news and bad news. The good news was that the company had not only survived but was actually coming out of the woods. The bad news was that all those who had pulled off this miracle were just about "Maxed" out.

I was working with OCF during this period, and during one session with a cross section of folks we were reviewing the state of the OCF Spirit. One word summed it up: dragging. When we got down to the question of what to do about it, I suggested, in almost an offhanded manner, that it would probably be useful to have a "Thank You Max Party," as a way of saying thank you to Max, and all the others who had put in the long hours, and also to mark a turning point to whatever it was that was to come next. Honoring the past and moving to the future, so to speak.

I had scarcely gotten the words out of my mouth when two young women, almost in unison, said, "We are going to do that." Interestingly enough, they did not say could we, should we, or may we, but "We are going to do that." It needs to be said that

OCF had virtually no female executives, senior or otherwise. The thought that two young women could make such an affirmative statement was fairly astonishing.

Their statement turned out to be the tip of the iceberg. In forty-eight hours they singlehandedly enlisted the interest and support of forty-plus people from all over corporate headquarters, established the time for a preliminary gathering, and were well on their way to doing something significant. Eight weeks from the day of their declaration, the Thank You Max Party, which by that time had been converted into the Pink Pride Rally, took place. Thirteen hundred people in pink T-shirts and drinking pink lemonade were regaled by the Pink Panther under six hundred pink balloons gathered beneath a huge banner that said thank you. For two hours they celebrated their past and looked toward the future.

That the party occurred at all was remarkable, but the way it came into being was even more surprising. Without formal budget, top-down approval, assigned staff, or any of the other standard necessities of getting things done in corporate America, these two young women made it all happen. Not that there weren't moments of anxiety, or even imminent disaster. But when zero hour arrived, the show went on.

How did they do it? Quite simply, they had a vision, held the vision, shared the vision, and grew the vision. And the vision became reality.

From the opening meeting until the opening gun, they operated superbly as mistresses of the informal organization. They began by telling a likely story of what it could/would be like, without worrying at the start about all the problems and reasons why it couldn't be done. When the story had grown rich enough so that the imagination of others was hooked, all those interested were invited to grow the collective tale.

At times it seemed like confusion twice confounded, and those with a more orderly streak were sure that nothing concrete would ever happen. But the organizers pressed on. Nobody was told what to do; rather, they were invited to contribute their best thoughts and actions.

Some of the suggestions were, by almost any standard, just plain crazy. But when those insane ideas were laid on the table of the organizing group (whose membership changed from meeting to meeting in confirmation of the First Immutable Principle), the proposers were honored, even as the ideas were seen to be a little off the mark. Indeed, it often seemed to be the rule that when a "crazy" idea was rejected, that merely opened the space for two sound ideas to be born.

A case in point was the matter of invitations. How would they get folks to come to the party? Standard procedure dictated approaching the CEO to receive his blessing and signature on an appropriate memo of invitation. The idea was deemed crazy for two reasons. First of all, it was by no means certain that the CEO would approve, and should he be asked and then disapprove, the whole thing was off. Equally important to the organizers was ownership of the rally. Were the invitation to come from the top, it would then be "their" party—not bad, but not quite what everybody had in mind. The party, if it were really going to work, would have to be "our" party. Solution? One of the young ladies took herself to the CEO's office and invited him.

Nobody had to come and nobody had to participate, either in the rally itself or in its preparations. But those who did come came from a point of passion. They had seen the vision, believed they could contribute, and taken personal responsibility for making their ideas a reality. As for the young women, they created the nurturant open space in which the story was grown collectively.

The significance of the event went far beyond having a good time, although that certainly took place. During a party to celebrate the Pink Pride Rally, folks had an opportunity to tell their stories and remember the highs and lows. The stories were told with animation, and they often concluded with words such as, "I really felt like I made a contribution, and I have never had so much fun in all the thirty years I have spent in this corporation, nor felt that my contribution was so worthwhile and appreciated" or "I really felt that I made a difference, but it was only a party."

When the last comment came by, about it being only a party, I asked, Was it? When was the last time you remember two young woman with no budget, formal authority, or management-selected team putting on a major shindig for thirteen hundred of your best customers? And all of that in eight weeks, from concept to delivery? I think you have done much more than a party—indeed, there is nothing you have done here that does not have immediate business application. OCF, like many corporations, has huge social gatherings for customers and clients, which may take a year and a million dollars to put together. The comparison was not only obvious but also odious.

Some other ground had been broken, too. The great myth of powerlessness had, in principle, been laid to rest. If two young women, one an accountant and the other a secretary, could do what they had done, nobody ever again could say, "I can't do that because I don't have the position power." There may of course be *many* good reasons not to do something (not appropriate, fear of punishment, and so on), but they are all *good* reasons and not *sufficient* ones. The power to make a difference is there if you choose to use it.

Last—but by no means least—is the issue of leadership. The case can be made that, certainly during the hours of the rally and those immediately preceding it, corporate leadership was in the hands of those two women. They did what neither the CEO nor Max had the power to do. They did it well and they made a difference. How long that difference would last was anybody's guess, but for a period Spirit was focused and liberated.

For those concerned with impact on the bottom line, the effect might appear minuscule. However, given the fact that prior to the rally there was mounting evidence that a number of important executives were not only exhausted but also beginning to look for a quick way out, and that after the rally the mood had palpably changed, one might argue that the bottom line effect was far from minor.

The Third Function of Leadership

Sustaining Spirit with Structure

Gathering and focusing Spirit is the first act of leadership, but if left at that point, Spirit will once again dissipate and disperse. Unless it is channeled for the long haul, Spirit raised by vision and fused in the collective story will fly apart. Organizational structure is the pathway of Spirit, and growing appropriate structure is the third function of leadership.

Creating organizational structure is probably what we in the West do best; at least we spend the most time on it. We pay a price for our fixation, however, for all too often structure is seen to be the only thing in an organization. At worst this leads to the denial of Spirit, which cuts us off from the true source of organizational power. Even under the best of circumstances, our obsession with structure causes us to build structure first and then to try to squeeze the Spirit into it. Architects understood some time ago that "form follows function."[1] In short, it is worthwhile to consider what you are going to do in a building before you build it. In a similar way, structure follows Spirit, and to reverse the order is to invite disaster.

Creating structure before attending to Spirit is like buying a pair of shoes without measuring your feet. It is possible that the shoes will fit, but it is much more likely that they will either pinch or fall off. Thus, while there are many possible organizational structures, there is no right one in the abstract; there are only *appropriate* ones—appropriate to the flow of Spirit in the particular organization.

The current fascination with round, flat, participatory organizations certainly has much to commend it, but it would be a mistake to think that steeply ranked, hierarchical structure is no longer ever appropriate. Hierarchies can and do work under circumstances where the quality of Spirit and the nature of the job at hand fit that particular way of being. For example, when putting out a fire with a bucket brigade, participatory management is not a good idea. Somebody needs to give the orders, and that person is usually the chief.

Not only is there no one right structure, but there also may actually be several useful ones, operational at the same time, as I discovered to my surprise while working with a client. When I first started working with this organization, I asked the CEO for a copy of the organizational chart. He smiled at my question, and just as I was about to say something about knowing that it was probably out of date, he broke in to tell me that they didn't have an organizational chart; they actually had about twenty of them. The organization's business involved some twenty different major projects, each having very different needs at different times. The organization had literally been reconfigured to fit the needs of each project and the needs of those who were going to do each job.

Although this approach might seem to be a recipe for confusion, my client had discovered that organizational charts were really useful for only two groups of people: customers and new employees. The former needed the chart in order to know who to call with a question, while the latter found it a useful security blanket while figuring out their place. Everybody else pretty well knew what was going on and felt quite comfortable concentrating on their job. So for every job there was a chart, available to the customer and to new employees. Because the customer was usually interested in only one job and the new employee would typically be working on only one job, the fact that there were other organizational charts was a matter of neither knowledge nor concern.

Growing Appropriate Structure

We may learn a lot about growing appropriate structure from the experience of those who built many of the new university campuses in the United States. It was often the case that these campuses, designed by landscape architects, were stronger on aesthetic appeal than on utility, especially when it came to walkways. The architects, seeking balance and symmetry (or whatever other design criteria they might have in their heads), laid out the walkways on which the students would presumably travel. After the campuses opened, however, it quickly became apparent that the elegant designs bore little relationship to the actual flow patterns of the students. The result was the creation of muddy pathways going in just about any direction except the ones the architect had in mind. The erection of fences and walls to channel the errant students usually had little effect, and what started out as a marvelous idea became a mess.

Then one day, a blinding flash of the obvious occurred: don't put in any pathways until you see which way the folks are going to travel. The initial period in this experiment was certainly a mess, but probably no worse than the alternative, in which the prescribed pathways were ignored while the adjacent lawns were destroyed. But given a little time, the tracks were laid down and all that remained was to pave them. Structure followed flow.

Building structure to fit and support Spirit is a laudable undertaking, but it requires the ability to "track" Spirit. Using the analogy of the college campus, how do we determine the footprints of Spirit in order to be able to pave the pathway into a serviceable all-weather road? The answer (surprise!) lies in the stories we tell.

A small consulting group tells a story about a mad dash to the airport. The offices of the group were located about five miles from the local airport, and as with many consulting groups, the airport was the beginning and the end of almost everything. On one occasion a senior consultant began the mad dash. With minutes to spare, he arrived at the airport only to discover that the nearby parking lots were full. There was nothing to do but throw caution to the wind, break the sound barrier—to say nothing of the local speed limits—and head for the satellite parking lot. The consultant quickly found a parking place, which fortunately was located near the bus stop. Wonder of wonders, a bus was there. Grabbing his bag, he raced to the bus, proud that he could still make his flight. But the driver had gone on a coffee break. The keys were in the ignition. Not wasting a moment, he settled into the driver's seat and drove to the terminal. Looking neither to the right nor to the left, he parked, and made his flight.

With stories like that, it is not difficult to sense the flow of Spirit in the consulting group, a flow that accomplished much but had little if any tolerance for elaborate, bureaucratic procedure. Not surprisingly, such structure that they had was honored mostly in its avoidance, and while they constantly vowed to get themselves organized, the truth of the matter was that they were well organized in a fashion that suited the flow of their Spirit perfectly.

Structure, Time, and Space

An organization's structure is the unique time-space configuration for that place. Within very broad limits, however, it is Spirit that defines time and space, and not the reverse. When it appears that Spirit has become a prisoner to time and space, that is typically a matter of choice or ignorance.

Obviously there are limits set by the duration of biological life and planetary existence. Sooner or later each of us will pass away, even as all of us will cease when the sun goes out. We do not have much choice about that, but the limits imposed are fairly broad.

By the same token, additional limits are imposed by other people's time and space, the structure of other constellations of Spirit. But the acceptance of those limits is always a matter of choice. By default or conscious intention, we choose the time and space in which our Spirit exists.

Most of the time, unfortunately, the availability of choice remains beyond awareness and we feel trapped. Occasionally this will create amusing situations, particularly when we realize how we have become our own worst enemies.

CREATING TIME

Several years ago, I was leading a five-day conference that was unusual by virtue of the fact that it had absolutely no formal agenda or timetable, except as the group of one hundred chose to create one. At the beginning, people knew only when we opened, when we closed, and the overall theme. This minimal format was, of course, Open Space Technology, and the occasion was the first instance of its use.

The conference began with an agenda-setting process in which all participants were encouraged to identify the areas of interest they would like to explore around the given topic. These interest areas were given short titles and posted on the wall, and all parties were invited to indicate their selection by signing up on the appropriate card. Time and space (where and when) arrangements were proposed by the initiators and negotiated with the potential participants. In something less than an hour and a half, the group of one hundred was ready for business.

The first day of the conference flowed with almost military precision. Working groups met at the times and places specified, and business got done. That evening, however, we had a small party, and the next morning the conferees were more than a little slow to line up at the starting gate. In fact, by the time we had all assembled, the official starting time of 9:00 A.M. had long since passed. And then, of course, coffee had to be drunk and morning greetings exchanged.

While all of this was taking place, I noticed one of the participants becoming more and more agitated. It seems that she had scheduled her group to meet at 11:00, and sensing the domino effect, she pleaded with me to stop all the chatter and get on with business. For reasons approaching "malice aforethought" I resisted her suggestion, if only because I felt that the coffee and morning greetings were essential to counteract the effects of the night before. The group finally got together at just about 11:00. As for the agitated participant, concern had given way to anger, with apoplexy near at hand.

When the time seemed right, I asked all the participants to take out their watches and announced that, for those who cared, the time was precisely nine o'clock. The immediate reaction was quizzical, followed by confusion, and eventually round-faced grins. *We had all learned that time is what you make it.* The Third Immutable Principle would apply: whenever it starts is the right time.

When Spirit is trapped in a time inappropriate to itself and the functions to be performed, the results can range from mild discomfiture to total system breakdown.

DIFFERENT TIMES

Western travelers to other cultures often find the nature of time there not to their liking. Everything (from the Western point of view) is late, slow, or never happens at all. Until one's internal clock is reset and one becomes used to the operative story ("*mañana*") and Spirit, the net result is no small amount of frustration, and occasionally disaster. By the same token, people from other cultures, attempting to operate under the Western sense of time, will experience similar difficulty.

Once I attended an international congress in Mexico on Organization Development. For reasons now obscure to me, the Mexicans had gotten the idea that to run a proper conference, they had to follow the Western rules. Accordingly, they prepared a statement of five "conference norms," which were prominently displayed on the screen at the beginning of the conference and at the start of each day. Among these norms was the announcement, "We will start all sessions on time."

It will not surprise any non-Westerner, or anyone who has worked in a non-Western environment, to learn that no session— not the first, the last, nor any in the middle—ever began on time. No matter how often the norm was enunciated, everything started when it was ready and not when the clock pointed to a particular hour.

What was surprising, or at least instructive, was that no matter when events started, everything of importance appeared to have been accomplished. In fact, more could have been accomplished had time not been spent trying to get everything to start on time. The conference had its own internal sense of rhythm, which was highly productive and had little to do with the clock. When I mentioned all of this to my hosts, they smiled enigmatically, but I did notice that as the conference progressed, the organizers began to treat the announcement more as a joke than as an expected behavior. In doing this, I believe they honored the "shape" of the conference Spirit with a time that was appropriate. At the very least, they became observably more comfortable with "their time" as opposed to the "right time," for their time was the right time.

MANY TIMES

The truth of the matter is that there are many times, each one appropriate to the Spirit of a given place and the job that needs to get done. With a little thought and effort it is quite possible to move from one time to another.

I am told that there is a small town somewhere in the American Midwest that for reasons of its own runs on two totally different times without problem. This particular town (as many such places) is laid out around the intersection of two highways, one running north to south, and the other running east to west. For half of the year the whole town runs on the same time, but come daylight saving time, things change because of the needs of the people and their work.

On the east side of town, a large dairy cooperative serves the local dairy farming community. On the west side of town, there is a small manufacturing plant that distributes its product all over the country. When daylight saving time comes in the spring, the west side of town makes the shift easily. Indeed, those who work in the plant have to shift in order to be aligned with their customers and suppliers, who are also on the new time.

Those on the east side of town, whose lives revolve around the dairy cooperative, have another consideration. While humans can easily switch the hands of a clock, cows operate rather differently. Milking time happens when it is time to milk. Thus the time in the east is milk time, not clock time. Daylight saving time never happens in the east, and the town has two times.

Under most circumstances, having two times is not a difficulty, except at lunch. It seems that the town's only restaurant is located at the highway junction, and for luncheon partners from opposite sides of the town it is essential to specify not only what time they will meet but also whose time they have in mind. So there has developed the local convention of "fast time" and "slow time." I can't remember which one is which, but all the locals can, and life moves in an orderly way. Time is appropriate to Spirit.

SPACE AND SPIRIT

Just as time is very often taken as a given, immutable reality, so also is space. Spirit may then become a prisoner of space instead of space being the appropriate site for Spirit and its activities.

Almost everyone has had the experience of walking into drab surroundings and feeling his or her spirit sag. When gray walls seem to close in from any point of view, the likelihood of spirited enterprise is remote indeed. But it is a mistake to presume that bigger is better, or that fresh paint will automatically make Spirit soar. While it is true that pleasant surroundings appear to have a positive impact on productivity, the connection is neither automatic nor necessary. The critical issue is always appropriateness.

A case in point was the glistening new office building that became the regional headquarters for Apex Corporation.[2] Apex was and is a dynamic, fast growing, high-tech firm specializing in computer applications for the military. Their original office facilities were notable for just about anything but glitz. They occupied cramped space over a Chinese laundry, across the street from Harry's Bar.

The history of the company's growth could easily be traced by observing the marks of old walls left indelibly imprinted in the floor. As projects came and went, walls were moved and space, albeit cramped, was created to meet needs. But no matter what was done, there never seemed to be enough space. People were falling all over each other, but surprisingly that condition was less a problem than a benefit. The close proximity turned out to produce a rich working environment in which productive interchange was almost inescapable.

The walls themselves became icons of history. Pert Charts, cartoons, and naughty and irreverent inscriptions bounded the space with colors and shapes unique to Apex's history. The highs and lows of past engagements served as reminders and challenges for the tasks at hand.

When really important work had to be done, requiring the best from everybody, Harry's Bar was more often than not the site of choice. What could not or would not get done in the normal working space moved across the street.

Then the decision was made to change the space. As it happened, a local real estate developer had some land on which he was prepared to erect the grandest building ever seen, at least in that part of the world. Seven stories tall, or thereabouts, with a soaring lobby and a glass-enclosed elevator rising in the center, it was nothing if not grand. But it certainly was not Apex.

Formerly close-working colleagues found themselves separated by whole floors, and even on the same floor running shoes were appropriate. Contrasted with the old situation, where everybody knew each other and what they were doing, the new building created an environment in which some people were frank to admit that they had never even been into the furthest reaches. And as far as knowing who worked there, that was beyond any direct knowledge. Harry's Bar, of course, was a thing of the past, and when people went out, they tended to disperse across the countryside in search of good food, regardless of the lack of good fellowship.

The move changed the Spirit at Apex. One might argue, of course, that the march of progress (if such it was) would quickly outweigh whatever discomfiture of Spirit had been created. And in the long term it may well be that the glorious new building would not only look more businesslike but would actually foster such behavior. In the interim, however, it was quite clear that Apex had lost a valued connection with its history. New employees would now enter an environment that looked a lot like every other high-tech organization. The special nuances, to say nothing of the mess, that made Apex Apex were nowhere to be seen.

CREATING POSITIVE SPACE

The creation of appropriate space for Spirit always begins with Spirit. Although aesthetic and other generalized design criteria apply, they must always be related to the Spirit of a place and not to abstract thoughts about the right way to do things. A strong example appeared during the closedown of a fifty-year-old plant.

The plant in question was located in southern California, and for more than half a century it produced a familiar line of products for a Fortune 500 corporation. In addition, it was the center of life for three generations. More than a job, the plant, and the associations that developed around it, created a social fabric that gave meaning and community to those who shared in it. From baseball games to skiing trips, life for many people began and ended with the plant. Then suddenly, the plant closed down. Rising real estate value and taxes coupled with stringent environmental restraints and an aging technology made it certain that the numbers would never come out right. It was nobody's fault particularly, and the decision to close was inevitable.

Unlike many plant closings, this one was done with a degree of humanity and intentionality that set it apart. A full fifteen months before the gates were to close, all employees were told what was going on.

In addition to providing the people with plenty of time to make the necessary adjustments in their lives, the company committed itself to a level of support during the process of transition that some might find unbelievable. Not only were people offered transfers or generous severance packages, but they were also provided with the time and guidance necessary to create their own futures. The plant manager intentionally created a learning community that became known as the University of the Future. Open to everybody, from senior managers to forklift drivers, the University of the Future provided the standard fare of classes on résumé writing and interviewing skills, and it went significantly beyond. Seminars were offered on organizations in transformation, transition management, creating small businesses, using your intuitive self, and a number of other topics that conventional wisdom might deem at or beyond the edge of the frivolous.

The University of the Future, and the Spirit engendered there, required space to happen. Part of the space was supplied by various hotels, where off-site seminars were conducted, but on the home campus the focal point was the Technical Skills Development Center. This center was located on a corner of the plant property and was fitted with offices and classrooms. It therefore seemed to be the only choice. Outplacement and training staffs were quartered there, and it was expected that people needing services would make the short trip across the parking lot to the facility.

That expectation turned out to be ill-founded, or at the very least the level of business was nothing like what might have been predicted. It was not that the place was uncomfortable, unattractive, or basically unsuited for the purpose. Rather, the trip across the parking lot was more than a short walk. For first timers, it ended up being the very long journey to the end of their careers at the plant.

Even though everybody knew that the plant would close and that the future lay elsewhere, that knowledge was exquisitely painful and not to be dwelled upon. For many, the pain of ending was such that a million reasons could always be found for not making the trip across the parking lot. And even when the trip was initiated, it was not uncommon to see it aborted halfway there. Walking through the parking lot almost guaranteed meeting friends, with whom it was all too easy to stop and pass the time while avoiding the sorrow. The center was the right place for many good and practical reasons, but it was not appropriate to the Spirit.

Another space offered itself, not so much by design as by happenstance, which is often the way with space fitting to Spirit. In the rush for closedown, a special order involving handpacking a large amount of the plant's product had been pushed further and further back on the agenda of things to do. That continued to be the situation until a young manager saw an opportunity in the problem. She had noticed that with the advent of closedown, and despite the operation of the University of the Future, time was hanging heavy on the hands of many employees. Worse than that, it was silent time. For reasons of embarrassment or fear, a lot of people simply were not talking through their plans and feelings. The manager reasoned that if she could just get people doing something together, the time would pass faster and they would also have the occasion to talk. So the MASH (Make Amazing Stuff Happen) project was born.

The actual arrangement was anything but business as usual. Everybody in the plant, from senior management on down, was invited to wrap product; indeed, they were often recruited as they walked in the door in the morning or on their way out at the end of the day. The only conditions were that folks must come in pairs. Upon arrival, participants were initiated into the MASH Team and given T-shirts as a sign of their union. Music, usually rock, formed the background, and decorations of all sorts festooned the otherwise drab environment. Prizes were to be awarded to the superwrappers, and the overall champion team would get the tape recorder on which the music had been played. When things started, Spirit was definitely up, and so it continued for the best part of a month. The product was wrapped in record time and, as predicted, people found the needed time to talk.

The MASH site became a magic place where people continued to gather long after the project had ended. When it came time to put on a job fair for those still looking for their next act, the MASH area was the site of choice. In retrospect, it is clear why that area became as powerful as it did. It was in the plant and not at the end of a long walk. It was familiar turf to everybody, although it had been made special by the decorations and the music, and most especially by virtue of the quality of Spirit that had been encountered there. By almost any standard, the MASH site would have been the last place to locate the University of the Future, but the truth of the matter is that it was, or became, totally appropriate to Spirit.

CREATING "THE BOOK":
SPACE OF A DIFFERENT SORT

The appropriate space for Spirit does not always have to be between four walls. It may also be between two covers. In the case of the plant closing, a book was designed to provide an opportunity for all to honor their past, consider their present, and shape their future.

When one thinks of writing a book, it is usual to name the theme, determine the structure, and gather the content, with a single person—otherwise known as the author—in charge. In this case, only the theme was named, and then everybody in the plant, even those who had left, were invited to contribute whatever they thought to be relevant under the general headings of Our Past, Our Present, and Our Future. The structure emerged from the content, and the "author" was a three-person editorial committee, who put it all together in two days.

Getting a large number of people to contribute to a book is no small task, particularly when they are divided by work shifts and the geography of the plant. The added pressures of closedown made it especially difficult. Thus a space of a different sort was required, which might be called electronic space. Utilizing the computer conferencing system of the corporation, which could be accessed through a large number of terminals in the plant or by phone from basically anywhere in the world, an anywhere-anytime space was created that people could enter at their pleasure. And enter they did. The offerings ranged from wonderful tales of the early days to thoughtful pieces reconsidering the approach to closedown in which the lessons being learned were summarized.

While "The Book," as it came to be known, would certainly not find a place on the bestseller list, it was probably more important to the people in the plant than a blockbuster could ever be. The Book represented the structured repository of the Spirit they had known during a most critical period of their lives. On the day the plant closed, copies were available for everyone.

CONCEPTUAL SPACE:
THE GEOMETRY OF OUR MINDS

The discussion so far has generally, and intentionally, avoided the more usual topics considered under the heading of organizational structure, such as organizational charts, chains of command, and the like. The primary reason is practical: it is much easier to illustrate the appropriateness of structure to Spirit with such earthy tales as MASH. But organizational charts, in whatever form, are also essential. They represent a different sort of space and time, which we might call "conceptual." Such things exists only in our thoughts, although the pieces of paper on which they are drawn can serve as useful reminders of what we had in mind. To speak of an organizational chart is to speak of a pure abstraction.

The geometry we hold in our minds, through which we understand the functions of our organizations, is potent indeed. And like more physical indicators of time and space, it as easily can become a *prison*, as an *aid* to Spirit. When our mental geometry describes a multilayered structure with checkpoints at every level, we will inevitably perceive "the top" as being a long way off and the journey there to be difficult and dangerous. Change that geometry into round or spherical, and suddenly all points become a lot more accessible. Transform the organizational geometry one more time, from single-centered to multicentered, and in an instant there is no longer a top or a center at all.

The permanence of the organizational geometry lies not in its abstraction but rather in its concrete application. Placing the CEO at the top of the organizational chart is very often made concrete by locating the executive suite on the upper floors of the building. At that point, the mental journey up the chart becomes a very physical one up the elevator or stairs. It may be that the view is better or that the space is more comfortable, but even when that is not the case, the mental geometry apparently persists. The executive suite of OCF, for example, occupies the twenty-eighth floor of a corporate office building in Toledo that has a nasty tendency to sway in high winds to the point of causing seasickness. Given the fact that Toledo is located but a short distance from the Great Lakes, from which the winds blow strongly and often, meeting senior staff displaying various shades of green is not an unknown experience.

Despite the fact that the geometry of the organization often assumes the permanence of stone, it remains an abstraction, useful when it channels Spirit in productive directions but stultifying or destructive when it does not. Should negative aspects appear, particularly when the structure has been cast in concrete and steel, it is natural but unnecessary to treat the result as an immutable given. Structure is, and remains, an abstraction from Spirit and therefore is changeable, even as the mind can change. And when the mind changes, even the corporate edifice can be altered.

Growing Structure: The Role of Leadership

If you consider the stories just presented about the emergence of appropriate structure (time and space) for Spirit, it may appear that structure was most effective when it arrived late. When problems arose, they were associated with preexisting or arbitrarily imposed structure. Thus, in the plant closedown, although the Skills Development Center possessed the requisite physical characteristics, it never really made it as the focal point for the University of the Future. Instead, the scruffy old shipping room became the critical center of Spirit.

One might also conclude that structure is not necessary, and that would be totally erroneous. Structure is the essential pathway of Spirit, but to fulfill that function it must always follow

Spirit's footprints; it must be appropriate to Spirit. Allowing and encouraging appropriate structure to emerge is a critical function of leadership, and one that cannot be undertaken lightly.

At this point, it is probably clearer what *not* to do. Above all else, do not impose structure arbitrarily. There is no such thing as the right structure, no matter what the current fads may suggest. The function of leadership is to *grow* structure, not to impose it. The process is an organic, evolutionary one, the work of a gardener, not a mechanic. Growing structure starts with Open Space (and Open Time), precisely the sort of space in which Spirit appears.

WORKING IN OPEN SPACE

Working in Open Space is not without its problems, particularly for those who equate leadership with control. For them it may appear that Open Space is nothing, and *how can you control anything with nothing?* This was four-star Admiral Harry Train's question as he became the executive director of Future of Hampton Roads (FHR) Inc. FHR Inc. emerged as the guiding organization from a massive project of Spirit-building undertaken in southeastern Virginia. In that part of the world, there are nine cities (such as Newport News, Norfolk, and Virginia Beach—the home of 1.2 million people) and four counties that had spent the better part of three hundred years either ignoring each other or in hostile combat. Eventually, a small group of private sector leaders came to the conclusion that they were shooting themselves in the foot. Although they sat on some of the finest real estate on the East Coast, little positive growth occurred because all the available energy was devoted to fighting. With some help from me, they resolved to make a change that involved creating a positive vision for the future and essentially telling a new tale for the region. How they proceeded is a long story, but succeed they did, with some very remarkable results.[3] For example, they managed to move their region from being rated the 149th marketplace in the United States into the top 50 category as number 29.

Early in this project, the community leaders created FHR as a base of operations and recruited the admiral to direct it. As Admiral Train and I were sitting outside the boardroom waiting for the board to make their selection official, he looked over at me and said, "Harrison, what have you gotten me into?" I am not sure that my answer really helped him but I said, "Well, Admiral, it is rather like being given the whole U.S. Army [which at that point had roughly 1.2 million people], which for its total history had been operating as thirteen autonomous and hostile units, with the assignment of getting all the troops together without a shred of line authority." "Oh," said the admiral. To his undying credit, the admiral succeeded beyond what even he would have admitted was the wildest of dreams. And he did it by learning to operate in Open Space.

Open Space is a far different beast, with very different rules, from the strict hierarchical structure the admiral had left as commander of the Atlantic Fleet, in which things supposedly got done through command and control. Open Space is an open space precisely because it is bounded. It is bounded by the central vision that establishes the context within which activity may take place. We are talking about *this* product and *this* market, as opposed to all others. Furthermore, the boundary of Open Space is strengthened and clarified as the collective story is woven, giving color and shape to what might take place. So, Open Space has a certain shape and location, if you will; but its critical quality is the absence of "a mess of stuff" inside.

Open Space stands as an invitation—a big, attractive, and doable invitation—for Spirit to enter and grow. There is, however, one fast and unfailing method for killing Spirit: to prematurely fill the space with a mess of stuff. Filling space is almost irresistible. Forget, for the moment, whatever needs leadership might be experiencing in terms of getting themselves organized and appearing to know what they are doing; the press from the outside is almost overwhelming. All those who have been attracted to the vision and empowered through the collective story will understandably want to get the show on the road. And more often than not they will want somebody to *tell* them what to do. The normal form for telling is a lengthy list of missions, goals, and objectives, set in a rigid timetable, with appropriate authority and responsibility established.

There will come a time for telling, but if it comes too soon the Spirit will die. Leadership must honor the space and avoid telling until it is the right time. Remember the Third Immutable Principle? There is no magic formula for determining the right time. It is always a fine judgment call, balanced between premature closure, which will kill Spirit, and unending delay, which will dissipate Spirit. But if there is any rule of thumb, it is something like, Wait as long as you can stand it, then wait just a little bit more. Nature abhors a vacuum, and people want to fill up Open Space with structure, so if error is to be made, err on the side of openness.

If vision is clear and the collective tale well told, the manifestation of structure will occur at the right time with amazing rapidity. Contrary to popular wisdom, which views the structuring of an organization as an unending, difficult task, it is almost pathetically easy when the conditions are right. For example, the forty-odd private sector leaders involved in FHR Inc. created an effective organizational structure for the organization in one day. Twenty-four hours later it was a legal entity with bylaws, bank account, and a board of directors. When the Spirit is up and clear, structure happens. Indeed, if there is any difficulty at all in the articulation of structure, that should be taken as prima facie evidence that the time was not right. Structural decisions, like good wine, spoil when taken ahead of their time.

FROM LEADERSHIP TO MANAGEMENT

When the time is right and structure emerges, the mode of operation passes from leadership to management. The importance of management, good management, cannot be overemphasized, but management has its place. Leadership liberates, management controls. Leadership operates in Open Space, and management operates the system. Leadership invokes and invites Spirit to lay down new footprints, management paves the path and keeps the troops on schedule and on the road.

Appropriate structure increases focus while removing eddies, distractions, and obstacles. It allows for all available energy to be targeted on the task at hand, which is what productivity and profits are all about. Rather than engaging in endless reinventions of the wheel, good structure and good management ensure that the task at hand is accomplished within resources and on schedule, with something left over for the bottom line. Management is essential.

It is worthwhile remembering that management works only in a given context and where there is general agreement as to what the context is. Should the context change or the agreement fail to exist, it is a whole new ball game. Managers control; that is their job. Control, in turn, depends on the ability to measure. As the old saw reminds us, "If you can't measure it, you can't manage it." Measurement, however, always depends on the context, from which it is calibrated. Place a Western manager in a Third World context and he or she will often complain that nothing happens on time. Right thought, but no agreed-upon context. The problem is not that things do not happen on time, but rather that there is not agreement on what time is.

Listening to current conversations, it seems that we may have gotten ourselves into a totally nonproductive discussion, even argument, about leadership and management. At worst it appears that one or the other is the only thing, and nothing could be further from the truth. In fact, leadership and management constitute a polarity, or continuum, that does not allow for either/or thinking. Both/and is the rule, although there are times when one side will predominate. In stable times, when environments tend to remain constant and systems are not constantly stressed or destroyed, management will inevitably be the dominant mode of operation. However, when the environment radically alters and systems are incessantly thrown into the chaos of Open Space, leadership must come to the fore.

We have experienced a number of years characterized by reasonable stability, and for understandable reasons management has been the dominant mode. The fruits of good management are everywhere apparent in the remarkable advance of productivity and efficiency. But it is safe to say that the times have changed and that the global context is being reset. At such a time we all experience the Open Space of ending and opportunity. The old structures give way, and time and space must be redefined to fit the new manifestations of Spirit.

All observable signs suggest that now is the time of leadership. And indeed, genuine leadership is required, but it must be leadership linked to good management. The rapid passage of events has so foreshortened the life cycles of our organizations that leadership and management must hold together. Conceptually this means abolishing the notion that there are leaders and managers. The fact that some individuals are more comfortable in one mode or the other does not obviate the necessity for each of us to lead and manage—while simultaneously being acutely aware of the context. As the context changes, so must the mode of our operation.

NOTES

1. Sullivan, Louis Henry, "The Tall Office Building Artistically Considered," *Lippincotts Magazine*, March 1896.

2. Apex is a pseudonym used to protect the innocent.
3. The details of this particular adventure are laid out in my book *Spirit* as the final case study.

The Fourth Function of Leadership

Comforting Spirit When Things Fall Apart

All good things come to an end. This is true of boxes of candy as well as outstanding human systems. To restate the Fourth Immutable Principle, "When it is over, it is over."

The second law of thermodynamics tells us that all systems tend toward entropy, which is a concise way of letting us know that eventually the energy that drives a system becomes so regularized and evenly distributed across the system that it is no longer clearly in evidence. Strange as it may seem, the first law of thermodynamics, which asserts that energy is neither created nor destroyed, is not contravened; for all appearances to the contrary, the energy is still there—it is just homogenized into sameness. There is no "difference that makes a difference."[1]

The same may be said about human systems. It is not that the originating Spirit has disappeared; it is only locked up in the organizational structure. What began as a flash of Spirit manifest in vision, focused through a collective tale, and made real and concrete in structure with its own time and space eventually becomes boring.

It is paradoxical to the extreme but the more perfectly an organization runs, the closer it is to its end. As structure is built and management refines and operates that structure, the level of efficiency and effectiveness, not to mention profitability, goes up. The driving Spirit that energizes an organization is channeled ever more narrowly into the task at hand. Nothing is wasted, nothing is spun off, and everything is focused on the bottom line, however that might be defined. The good news is that the machine works well. The bad news is that it is boring.

OCF was a superbly managed organization. It dominated the market it had created with the invention of its major product, it was profitable to a fault (which made it a tasty takeover target), and it seemed to many that the company would simply last forever. But when I interviewed a number of executives in those halcyon days before Wicks, I discovered a curious and constant refrain in the stories they told. On the one hand, they were quick to acknowledge the positive. Their compensation was adequate, training and development programs were constantly available, and a well-defined and smoothly functioning reward system was in place, but. . . .

But? Who could ask for anything more? What possibly could be missing from this picture of general perfection? The answer usually came in words like, "But, you know, we haven't had any fun in ten years."

Somehow the excitement and adrenaline surges of the "old days" had disappeared. The good news was that the system worked, and worked exceedingly well. The bad news was, it was dull. The pathways for Spirit in that place had been so carefully laid out and maintained (not to mention guarded) that there was no sense of adventure.

Having fun on the job has not, until recently, been understood as an essential working condition, but to tell the truth, when the fun and excitement stop and boredom sets in, a number of other definitely less desirable effects are almost certainly in the wings. Boredom inevitably produces sloppiness and troublemakers, a fact well known to parents and nursery school teachers.

Bored employees tend to overlook the details, which translates directly into a decline of quality and an increase in customer dissatisfaction. Boredom also gives birth to troublemakers, for the Spirit is still there, it is just feeling claustrophobic. Trouble, of course, can come in many packages. At best it will emerge as harmless pranks, done just to make the time go faster. At worst, trouble comes in packages labeled office bickering, backbiting, nasty rumors, and worse.

Boredom also manifests itself in a decline in creativity. I do not know it to be a fact but the story at OCF was that they hadn't had a truly new product in ten years, during a time when they maintained an enormous research facility on a two hundred-acre campus with twelve hundred employees.

OCF, to its credit, was by no means blind to these disturbing symptoms. Their response, very much in line with general corporate practice, was an attempt to fix the system. The fix went in two directions. On the one hand, there was a heavy investment in quality control: checkers to check the checkers, guided by a superchecker. On the other hand, programs were introduced to raise creativity, most particularly an outstanding import from Sweden created by the Foresight Group and known as the School for Intrepreneurs. The school represented an honest attempt to juice up the old system with a good shot of entrepreneurial zeal.

The Wicks takeover intervened before all these fixes could be fully played out; but had Wicks not come onto the scene, I strongly suspect that the experience at OCF would have paralleled that of all other organizations I know under similar circumstances. The proposed system fixes would not have worked; indeed, they would have been counterproductive. The problem was not that the system wasn't working, but precisely the opposite. The system was doing exactly what it was designed to do—channel Spirit. In doing its job it was also reaching its intended goals, which were efficiency, effectiveness, and profitability. There were, unfortunately, some toxic by-products.

Under the circumstances, the proposed fixes really would not have done much good. The increase in quality control would only have further tightened the system and increased the constraints on available Spirit. In practical terms, the results would appear as reduced flexibility and increased costs—not exactly what was needed.

As for the School for Intrepreneurs, the intent was laudable but the outcome could have been disastrous, for as the program released entrepreneurial zeal, even as the system moved toward greater control, something would have had to give. It is possible that the rising young intrepreneurs really would have made a difference, in which case the system would have been radically altered. More likely, the system would have triumphed, and it would have been back to business as usual. Neither effort could have altered the fact that when it is over, it is over.

The advent of Wicks, with its hostile takeover attempt, short-circuited the process and may well have saved OCF, but it was certainly not the OCF that used to be. In the days and months following the tender offer, there was a great deal of conversation about the "new" OCF. Admittedly there was not a high level of agreement about what the new OCF would be, but I think it was apparent to all that the old OCF had gone.

Also apparent was an outbreak of Spirit. Although the time immediately surrounding the takeover attempt was painful indeed, resulting in enormous disruption in the lives of many people, it surely was not boring. Candid conversations often yielded statements like, "It surely has been rough, but truth to tell, I haven't had so much fun in years. Talk about challenge and performance! It was exciting to know that our corporate life was on the line, which meant that we all had to make a difference."

Even those who left seemed to share some of the excitement, as I found out indirectly from a message left on my answering machine by the son of a former executive. This young man told me that his father was a terminated OCF executive. After thirty years with the company the shock of termination was no small thing, but when the anger and pain cleared, his father discovered a remarkable thing. He had been imprisoned by a system that had taken all his time, energy, and talent. When it all broke down, he climbed on a plane to go visit his son. They talked seriously for the first time in twenty years.

Why Wait for Wicks?

If it is true that there is a certain naturalness of ending and that inevitably there will come a time when a system has not only fulfilled but also exhausted its potential, why is it that we sit around until the inevitable is obvious? Why indeed?

There are probably a million ways to candy-coat the answer, but none of them will avoid the final conclusion. We wait because of death: we don't like it. The extremity of this statement is not meant for shock value, but rather to bring the discussion quickly to where it needs to be. Using the word *death* may appear to be an overstatement, but I seriously believe it is what we experience when our systems reach their end. In a plant closing or a major downsizing, one has only to visit briefly with with those walking out the door, as well as with those who remain, to understand the depth of the situation. If it is not death, it is surely the next thing to it. Good "company folks" who spent all of their working lives going to the same place, doing the same thing, hoping the common hope and expecting the common reward are finished.

For better or worse, we define ourselves by what we do. Small children understand this immediately when with pride or confusion they say, "My Daddy or Mommy does. . . ." At a cocktail party or in a bar, the answer to the question "Who are you?" is as likely to be your title or profession as your name. And when that definition no longer applies, life as we once knew it isn't anymore.

Of course there are those for whom a job is just a job, and they will walk out the door with no further thought. But such people are not, nor will they ever be, the heart and soul of an organization. They just fill a slot, anchor a desk, and pass the time. We say of them that their heart is not in it, which means that there is no danger of their losing heart when it is all over. Doubtless there is a place for such people, but should they assume a majority position, the organization is in deep trouble.

Without heart there is no commitment, loyalty, and all the other good things that make an organization fly. But with heart, commitment, and loyalty comes attachment. When attachment breaks, pain results. You may not want to call it death, and may choose another word, but experience has taught me that *the human reaction is the same, no matter what the name.* When it is over, it is over, and that hurts.

Speaking of a system ending as dying not only fits the circumstances but also brings us to a point where we can talk honestly about the factors involved in our inability to face the situation early on and proactively. The issue is not lack of knowledge, for we have all known since childhood that what goes up must come down, that what begins will end, and that sometime we will each cease. However, having the knowledge and being able to deal with it are two separate things. Indeed, we in the West expend extraordinary effort distancing ourselves as far as possible from the reality of death. Until fairly recently, even talking about dying was considered poor form. The cosmetic industry makes a fortune helping us all to pretend that those early indicators of approaching demise are not there. And the funeral business seems to be about masking the reality of dying so that the corpse looks more alive than the living. Our language continues the charade, for few, if any, ever die. They pass on, fall asleep, go to the other side, take the trip. Nobody dies.

Corporate executives are no less averse to the downside. Everything must be "beginning" and "new," with no thought of ending or passing from the scene. Annual reports are replete with success stories and new ventures, but the ones that have ended warrant only a footnote, if they are mentioned at all. Consultants and trainers are equally guilty, offering magic bullets for the attainment of power (read excellence), but nary a word about what to do when it all falls apart. This may be shortsighted, but it is quite understandable, for who would pay to be told that all good things come to an end? It is surely better to remain in ignorance, even pretended ignorance.

In this case, ignorance is not bliss, and certainly not when the inevitable becomes reality. But it is no wonder that the end of a system, organization, or corporation always seems to come as a surprise, with absolutely no advance preparation.

Leadership and Making a Good Ending

The Japanese have a curious concept that they call "a good death." To Western ears this is a complete, oxymoronic contradiction. How could death possibly be good? Leaving aside the details for the moment, the mere existence of the phrase points out that there are some different ways of looking at death and ending. Both of these realities may be viewed as the total cessation of everything, in which case our typical way of dealing with them makes a great deal of sense. If you can't do anything about something, and it doesn't make any difference anyhow, best to put it as far out of your mind as possible and get on with the business of the moment.

Should it turn out, however, that ending is simultaneously the fulfillment and the fracturing of finite forms (in this case, human systems, be they corporations or something else), then avoiding the end is avoiding the meaning and purpose for which something was created. In other words, evading death usually results in avoiding life. Indeed, individuals and organizations who drink it all down to the dregs are precisely the ones who live life in full measure.

There is yet another thought hidden in the idea of a good death. Endings are the necessary precursors to new beginnings. One simply cannot get on with whatever is coming next until and unless the present passes. This thought suggests that in avoiding the fact of ending and death, one misses out not only on the fulfillment of present reality but also on the opening of the next act.

These "hidden thoughts" suggest some added dimensions to leadership. We have previously seen the critical role that leadership plays in creating and maintaining the Open Space in which Spirit appears, first in vision, then in collective storytelling, and in the last chapter, when structure is grown. We now face the ultimate Open Space—when everything falls away. Leadership must be there at the end.

When a human system, particularly a business or part of a business, shows the unmistakable signs of ending, the sequence of behavior at the top is, unfortunately, fairly predictable:

1. Ignore it, perhaps it will go away.
2. Deny it, perhaps it isn't so.
3. Find somebody else to blame, so at least you do not get tagged with the failure.
4. Bail out as quickly as possible with the largest parachute available.

Given the current infatuation with success, coupled with an inability to deal with death (our own or that of others), this behavior not only makes sense but it also is the only behavior possible. The cost, however, is enormous. In individual human terms, such behavior means that at precisely the moment when Spirit needs to be supported and cared for, those who should assume that responsibility disappear. The pain of ending is real and the despair engendered is inescapable, but if that pain and despair are not to last forever, someone, or several someones, must assume the mantle of leadership, to stand in the middle, just to be there and listen. Not a pleasant task, but I think it comes with the territory.

There are additional organizational costs chargeable to the present behavior of many who call themselves leaders. If the time of ending is also the time of fulfillment, what better learning opportunity could possibly present itself to reflect on all that has been done, as a basis for doing it better or differently? When business ceases, there is time to see, with a clarity unavailable previously. Closing one's eyes or bailing out at a time of learning is exceedingly wasteful. Obviously this is not a task for the faint-hearted, but nobody ever said leadership was going to be easy.

Endings and New Beginnings

There was a time, of course, when it seemed that our organizations would go on forever. Incremental changes might come and go, but the expectation was "our corporation forever." Of course there were always those moments when really big changes came along, but they seemed few and far between and could largely be handled by that convenient mechanism I call the Generational Flush. Once every twenty years or so, all the old guys retired, died, or were otherwise pushed aside. At that time, new blood could come in, along with new ideas and approaches. This was known as "progress by funerals," and in the interim there was not much to do but wait your turn.

We no longer have the luxury to wait for the Generational Flush. Whole businesses—indeed, even industries—come and go within a few years. Maintaining the competitive edge, to say nothing of simple existence, requires that we do in a decade what many before us never had to negotiate in a lifetime. And we can only believe that the pace we experience will increase. If it is not true that all endings create the Open Space within which new beginnings can occur, we better make it so, or throw in the towel right now.

Converting endings to new beginnings obviously requires more than wishing it were so. For when the end comes, Spirit sags, slips away, and sometimes just plain goes over the hill. New beginnings require new Spirit, or at least getting the old Spirit back together again, which poses the interesting question, How do you raise Spirit?

NOTE

1. Gregory Bateson, *Steps to an Ecology of Mind* (New York: Ballantine, 1972).

The Fifth Function of Leadership

Raising Spirit

Raising Spirit is the final task of leadership. It is final in the sense that it is the last one on the list of leadership functions, and also because it represents the critical difference between continuation and ultimate demise.

When an organization simultaneously reaches its fulfillment and its end, the old forms, structures, building, plants, and facilities may persist for a period, indeed even hundreds of years, but they are rather like the remains of former civilizations—empty shells in which life was lived. There may be a few caretakers, hangers-on, and remnants of former days, but the Spirit of the place moves out pretty quickly.

Separated from the ruins of ancient Greece or Egypt by several millennia, we may look at them with a certain equanimity, even nostalgic attachment. But when the ruins happen to be your organization or business, such dispassionate contemplation is not likely. Leaving aside all elemental questions about the necessity to earn a living, certain thoughts will inevitably appear about all that might have been done, or that could still be done, if the Spirit were available. Question: How do you revive Spirit, not in the same old form, but in new forms and new structures appropriate to the changing environment?

The work of Ilya Prigogine, referred to in Chapter Two, offers some suggestions and even hope. As you will remember, Prigogine tells us that systems stressed by a changing environment will move further and further out of equilibrium, seeking to readjust their present form to the new circumstances. Their activity will appear chaotic and random, and as the stress levels increase, so will the crazy efforts at adjustment. Finally, when no further adjustment is possible, the system will either fly apart or literally "pop" in a radical, discontinuous jump to new and more appropriate ways of being in that environment.

If the first part of Prigogine's description sounds rather like a human system at the end of its rope—or more concretely, like your business when the competitors have just dropped a real bomb or the stock market has crashed—it may also be true that there is a pop in your future. And pop beats flop every time. But the question remains: How do you engineer such a thing?

Were it necessary to create an effective approach de novo, I suspect that it might be a long time in coming. But the truth of the matter is that the mechanism already exists, and that we as a species have worked with and through it from our beginning. In contemporary literature, that mechanism is called *griefwork*, but other ages and traditions would give it a different name. It is the period of mourning, the wake, the requiem, or sitting Shiva.

Griefwork is what we human beings do when confronted by death, our own or the death of another. Virtually all modern research in this area has related to the individual response, but in my experience, precisely the same patterns take place when a whole organization is in jeopardy.[1] What we now know of the process enables us not only to understand and predict with some accuracy the course of events under very trying and tumultuous circumstances, but also to identify and facilitate critical points along the way. Whatever else leadership may be about, surely it finds its center of meaning when the chips are down, quite literally, and it is time to raise Spirit.

Before moving on with the hows and whys, I must once again make it exquisitely clear that in using the word *leadership* I do not refer to the leader, titular or otherwise, who in his or her own power is expected to pull off all of this. Altruistic and democratic principles aside, there is absolutely no possibility that any one person could accomplish what needs to get done. Recall two of the new rules of leadership introduced in Chapter Three: *The leader is whoever has the ball*, and the corollary to that, *Ball hogs die*. I believe that these rules always apply, but particularly in those moments when Spirit is dragging and must be raised up. The complexity of events, coupled with the strain and stress of the situation, requires that each person be leader to the others. We all make it together, or nobody makes it at all.

Grief at Work

The experience of grief is known to us all in those moments when a loved one dies, a relationship ends, or a lifework is over. That lifework may be your individual life, or a life defined in and through a particular organization, but the feeling of loss and the act of grieving will take place in any case.

What most of us experience as an intense feeling is also a constructive process through which we honor the past, acknowledge the present, and set off for the future. It is our way of gathering our Spirit and moving to a new form. The power of the process is such that in its midst it is difficult, perhaps impossible, to know anything other than that it began, it continues with pain, and eventually it ends. In fact, there are definite stages along the way, and although that knowledge may do little to ease the immediate pain, recognizing the stages as they pass can do much to orient you and help you to help others.

Griefwork begins with the moment of ending or its imminent approach. Its first manifestation is *shock and anger*. The response is purely physiological and is nothing more than breathing in and

---

THE STAGES OF GRIEF AT WORK

Shock and anger

Denial/If only

Memories

Open Space

Imagination

Vision

---

breathing out strongly—as in "Ooooooh, damnnnn!" The good news is that the patient is still breathing, and in moments of shock the cessation of that life-giving function is a real possibility. But as a long-term strategy it does little more than keep life going and the Spirit alive until something else can be done.

First aid is administered by the next step, which I call *denial/ if-onlies*. Denial is the pretense that nothing has happened, that life will surely go on as it always has. In an organizational setting, denial is expressed in words like, They can't close this plant down. How are those idiots on the other coast going to serve the whole region?

When that kind of masking no longer works, the *if-onlies* start, as in, "If only we had done something sooner—listened to that consultant/not listened to that consultant." The reality is, it is all over, but denial and the if-onlies serve to push the pain off to a safe distance. In themselves they do absolutely no good in terms of materially altering the situation, but what they do accomplish is critical. They provide distancing and surcease from the intense pain of ending—just what a bandage does for the healing of a wound.

As the irreversible reality of the situation sinks in, although we are somewhat numbed by the anesthesia of denial, the healing process begins in earnest; but here as in many points in life it is necessary to go backward in order to make progress. The mechanism is *memory*. In the vacuum of ending, the memories flow through, with thoughts of all the things that were and are no longer, that might have been, and that can never be. The sweet ones, the sad ones, the mad ones, the bad ones—all pass in review. For those watching this stage, it may well seem like a useless and interminable retreat to the past. Verbally it will sound much the same as the previous stage of denial, but there is an important difference. Whereas denial was living in make-believe, the passage of memories is a serious acknowledgment of the past, with the clear recognition that it is gone. Far from being useless, this acknowledgment is essential to honoring and releasing the past before the future ever becomes a possibility. The story, which bounds Spirit, is being rewritten and prepared for a new tale that will be told.

After a while, memories slow and eventually cease. There is nothing more to say. All the heroes have been identified and the major events reviewed. What remains is silence and pure Open Space.

This Open Space is initially experienced as being profoundly down in the dumps, bereft of anything. Call it despair, for it is the empty agony of ending. There is nothing left, nothing to do, and no hope of bringing it all back again. Neither anger, denial, nor memory can restore what is no longer. It is over.

If the pain is intense, there is also a sweetness in that pain, reminiscent of the first snow in early winter. The summer is past. The leaves lie dead on the ground. In the silence, the first flakes fall. There is profundity and awesomeness in that moment of silence—a holy moment, a moment filled with wholeness[2] and completion. In the absence of all the things that should be done, could be done, or might be done, one finally can confront the searing questions: Why do anything at all? What is really important? What is worthwhile doing? What does it all mean anyhow?

"Nothing" may be the answer returned. If that is so, there is little to do but acknowledge the obvious as Spirit goes on its way. This is difficult to do, but it is essential to honor that answer, no matter what other plans might be affected. Even if it were possible to plead and cajole, appealing to corporate loyalty, family pride, or whatever else may have persuasive power, a verbal turnaround would do little good. When one has looked into the depths and seen no future, there is no meaningful leverage. Nothing times nothing is, unfortunately, nothing. With nothing to give and nothing to gain, nothing will be accomplished.

But there is another possible outcome should despair turn to *imagination.* In the silence of ending, when there is nothing left to be done, the ground is cleared of all the *shoulds, oughts,* and *musts.* It is now possible to think of the *might-bes,* and the *what-ifs.* No longer constrained by what was, everything now becomes possible. Pure possibility is the seedbed of imagination.

Imagination cannot be forced, but it may be invited, even as Spirit will not be coerced but may be invoked. The proper invitation to imagination is not to issue the next five-year plan or provide the full-blown description of coming attractions. The invitation is always a question. The form may be various, but the substance will always be something like, *What are you going to do for the rest of your life?*

Questions maintain the Open Space within which imagination and Spirit can grow. The power of the questions lies in their capacity to evoke, creating a sense of futurity, the mere possibility that the end is not all and that beginning is at hand.

An invitation extended is no guarantee of acceptance, but if Spirit enters and imagination is sparked, it will become manifest in statements like, "You know, the old organization was really grand, but we never could quite reach the potential I'd hoped for.

I wonder if. . . ." Imagination plus wonder creates vision, from which futures are made.

Thus we have completed the cycle, returning to the moment from which we began, when Spirit is evoked by vision. But if the journey has been an effective one, Spirit renewed is not the same old thing with fresh paint. As the old vision, collective story, and structures of time and space fall away, victim to a changing world, new manifestations of Spirit emerge—related for sure, but now appropriate to a changed world. The process of transformation moves on.

Leadership and the Process of Grief

Whatever else leadership may be able to accomplish, it cannot do griefwork for anybody. That, fortunately or unfortunately, is something that individuals must do for themselves, even if they all do it together. Nor can leadership minimize the pain or somehow protect those who grieve from their grief. Humanitarian concerns may strongly suggest the opposite, and when those concerns are blended with holdovers from the present dominant view of leadership, the temptation to intervene may become almost irresistible. But resisted it must be, first because it is useless, but most importantly because the mere attempt at intervention may retard or abort the process, a process through which individuals and organizations evolve and transform. No pain, no gain.

The mention of "holdovers from the present view of leadership" probably needs elaboration. As long as leadership is viewed as the exclusive prerogative of the one or the few, to be exercised for the benefit (or detriment) of the many, the basic mode of relationship between leaders and followers will be some form of passive dependency. At worst this means treating followers as "those idiots," although advanced leaders in the old mode seem to be moving toward an enlightened paternalism or maternalism.

The master-servant relationship may work well in more ordered times, and for sure it does wonderful (albeit superficial) things for the egos of leaders and the security needs of followers, but when the times become chaotic, the relationship is not only unworkable, it is also counterproductive. At precisely the moment when all of us must take maximum responsibility for ourselves, that responsibility is denied. No one can negotiate the path of transformation for another.

Obviously there are cases of real need and genuine incapacity (mental, physical, and social), but when incapacity is presumed, that presumption often becomes a self-limiting and self-fulfilling prophesy. So the issue is not a matter of absolute do's and don'ts but rather of presumptions. Presume incapacity and it will likely be found or created. Presume capacity for responsible action and you may well be surprised. In no event, however, can our presumptions change reality. Negotiating the process of transformation is something that can never be done for another person. Transformation, like death (because it involves death), is a solo activity. In the words of the old spiritual, "You got to walk that lonesome valley by yourself."[3]

Love: What Leadership *Can* Do

Leadership in the process of grief, or more broadly, in the course of transformation, is critical, but it does not play out according to the old rules. *The prime function of leadership is to love*, and to manifest that love by (1) really being there at the end, (2) maintaining the Open Space, and (3) evoking The Question.

THE TWO FACES OF LOVE

The word *love* is used in so many ways as to have almost lost its meaning, referring to everything from raw fornication to some idealized state, and even to the Divine Being (as in "God is Love"). Perhaps the normative use is *acceptance.*

I am clear that love includes acceptance, but I believe there is more. Love, in my experience, always has two faces, a face of acceptance *and* a face of challenge. It is never either/or; it is always both/and, and the power of love is manifest in the Open Space created by the two faces.

The first face of love is *unconditional acceptance*—taking others just the way they are, where they are, and how they are, with no questions asked. It is nonjudgmental to a fault. The good news of acceptance is that when we find ourselves accepted, we can more easily accept ourselves as we are—no justification, no rationalization, no apologies. But acceptance has its downside. Without standards, life turns to mush. Without rigor, thinking becomes sloppy. Without judgment, anything goes. Pure acceptance leaves you just where you are and never urges you to become everything you could be.

The other face of love is *radical challenge,* a challenge potentially so extreme that you are catapulted into new ways of being. The standards are set, the expectations are there, the judgment is real. Mushy life won't do. Sloppy thinking is unacceptable. Challenge is the road to fulfillment. But challenge by itself is disastrous, for it creates a life of unmitigated harshness.

THE OPEN SPACE OF LOVE

Neither face of love will work alone. Although we may prefer the comfort of acceptance, and it certainly is comfortable, we require the stringent slap in the face of challenge. But it must always be challenge grounded in acceptance, and acceptance excited by challenge. In personal terms, we may address each other as follows: "I take you just the way you are and expect you to become everything of which you are capable—and more."

Love is neither acceptance nor challenge alone; rather, it is the Open Space created by the tension between the two. Maintaining that tension (dialectic, polarity, call it what you will) is no easy task. It is always tempting to give in to the comfortableness of acceptance, or to lose patience and issue an ultimate challenge. But the depth of love is measured by the breadth of the Open Space. *Partial love* is one or the other; *little love* is marginal acceptance and minimal challenge; *great love* is acceptance and challenge without boundary.

Although this notion of Love may appear different, and perhaps strange, it is not without precedent. In Indian mythology, the two faces of Shiva (destroyer and creator) create the same polarity. From the Tao comes the yin and the yang, to the same effect. And in the Torah (Old Testament to the Christians) there is Yahweh's (God's) *mishpat* (judgment) and *chesed* (loving kindness) appearing in and through His essence, which is love (*Ahabh*). Those traditions, at least, understand mankind to reach fulfillment in the presence of the love of god or gods, and that love is always manifest in the polarity of acceptance and challenge.

Leadership, Love, and Grief

When the end comes and grief commences, loving leadership is essential, and that love will manifest itself in some very concrete ways, by really being there, maintaining the Open Space, and evoking The Question.

BEING THERE IN LOVE

The first and possibly the most difficult manifestation of love is to be there, right in the middle of all of the grief and chaos. Not just as a visible body, although that may be the only possibility sometimes, and certainly physical presence is usually better than none at all. But being there means really being *there,* accepting the folks and the reality of ending just the way it is, while simultaneously expecting and urging the new reality into being.

In more specific terms, this means being open and available to everything—the pain, the tears, the loneliness, the feelings of self-doubt, the intimations of meaninglessness. As a leader, you can't change any of that, nor can you ultimately (or proximately) shield your fellows from the searing effect. Your presence is made more difficult, not to mention painful, by the same feelings in yourself. But leadership at a distance is not possible. As Harry Truman is reported to have said, "If you can't stand the heat, get out of the kitchen."

None but a fool would underplay the cost of such proximity. When the tears of others become your tears, when their fear is your own, the effect is not pleasant. It might be made more bearable were you able to maintain an Olympian distance, but more often than not that escape route is denied for the simple reason that the tears of others are, in fact, your own, even as the fear is held in common. Unless you just dropped in from some other planet, you are all going through it together.

If the cost is steep, the reward is higher. As the process of grief works its way through from anger to denial, past memories, down into the dumps, and on to imagination, and then to vision, dissolution turns to triumph, chaos to order.

All of which brings up an interesting question: How do you stand it? For those who persist in playing by the old rules, the answer is stark: you can't. If there is any lingering thought that the leader can and must always be in control, taking everything onto himself or herself, truly being there is not possible. Sooner or later that sort of leader will find it necessary to take a quick trip to the executive suite, never to be seen again—or if seen, then always through some safe protective shield, the "official appearance," as it were.

Sticking it out "in the kitchen" is never something that can be done alone. The idea that we all must be leaders to one another is a matter not of democratic ideal but of practical necessity. Under the extreme conditions of transformation, in the middle of the process of grief, it is inescapably true that the leader is *whoever has the ball*—and for sure, *ball hogs die.*

MAINTAINING OPEN SPACE

The task of leadership at the onset of the process of grief is to do nothing, or certainly as little as possible. No schedules can be set, lectures given, MBO's (Management By Objective) prepared. If no *thing* can be done, however much must be accomplished under the heading of creating space: establishing the time, place, and permission to get on with the business.

The initial stages of grieving simply have to roll out, and leadership must see that the opportunity is available for all that to occur. Above everything else, it is imperative to recognize that there is no possibility of arbitrarily shortening the process or skipping stages. Shock and anger are there and must be expressed and accepted. Allowing for a collective "Ooooooh, damnnnn" or the equivalent is essential. No attempts to muffle the noise, to make things seem polite and proper, or to downplay the intensity of feeling with soothing words of consolation will have any useful effect. Indeed, they will be completely nonproductive. Shock not followed by anger usually means that breathing has stopped. And anger unexpressed inevitably goes underground to eat out stomachs and poison future working relationships.

The same is true with denial. Although cooler and more rational heads will see that the pretense of continued denial is only make-believe, the anesthetic quality of denial is critical to the moment. No exhortations to "deal with reality" will change the fact that at the moment reality is too painful to be dealt with. Some people never will deal with the reality of ending, and they will be lost to the possibility of new beginning, but even they must be given the space to make that choice. Nobody can do it for them, nor can it be done before they are ready. When it is time, it is time, and not before.

When grief moves us to deal with memories, the role of leadership can become more overt by creating special times and places, even formalized ones, where memories can be honored. This is the function of the Irish wake, but you don't have to be Irish to gather the benefits. A special time to honor the heroes and salute the mighty deeds, all in the context of a dinner and a glass or two, won't hurt. But no matter what, *do not stop the process.* Heros unsung and deeds not honored will surely lie restless in the grave and never become available to inspire the evolving future.

Honoring heroes is best done with love. It is essential that they and their deeds be taken at face value. For only in doing that can we really appreciate, for better or worse, what has transpired. But dealing with heroes only at the level of acceptance is not sufficient, for then we never ask what could have been done. What are the possible implications of their contributions? The function of memories, as grief works, is not only to let go of the past but also to lay the groundwork for whatever comes next. It is the front edge of a learning process that can take us from where we were toward whatever we might become. And the driving engine of that process is critical judgment. Love maintains the Open Space in which heroes can be seen for what they were, and learned from, as a guide to possible futures.

A truly profound moment for leadership appears in the depths, when the memories have passed and the silence of ending is deafening. The temptation to break that silence will prove almost irresistible, but if yielded to, the moment will be lost. For concealed in that moment are the seeds of the future, which must be allowed to germinate. In the clarity of ending, when everything else is gone, comes the extraordinary opportunity to consider what it all means. Don't waste it. Honor the Open Space with the dignity of silence. In that silence, wonder may appear.

ASK THE QUESTION

There will come a time when wonder turns to imagination, but leadership cannot rush to fill in the details. The critical point is The Question: *What are you going to do with the rest of your life?* The posing of that question will mark the shift from ending to new beginning, and it is the unique task of leadership to sense the moment when The Question is ripe. No magic formula applies here, and clock time is entirely useless, for the question will set its own time; indeed, time will start anew with the posing of The Question.

It would be a consummate error to suppose that at this point leadership by the old rules may now reemerge, with the leader lining up the troops to await their answer. The question will be asked by all of us to each of us in a thousand different ways. It may be quite direct, or more often than not the critical question will be posed in the beckoning rays of a dawning sun, suggesting that a new day might just come; or it may be in the hungry cry of a newborn child, reminding us that life begins anew. Each of us has different ears and different eyes, but all of us may become leaders to one another by offering The Question in ways that may be seen and heard.

Asking The Question in love is the deepest act of leadership. For just as The Question creates the space within which the quest for new life may be pursued, it is love that releases the Spirit for the journey. Love as acceptance creates the conditions in which things may be taken just the way they are, allowing the realization that it really is over. We really can let go and move on. Love as challenge points the way, not with a detailed plan that must be followed but rather with the expectation of future fulfillment.

Do We Really Have to Go Through All This?

Doubtless there are times when we might wish that the ruler of the universe had consulted us prior to setting up the original design, for surely we could have figured out a better way. But in fact I strongly suspect that the Great Cosmic Being (by whatever name) has already given us precisely what we are asking for. For better or for worse, we have been left with the responsibility for deciding and designing what we are to become. But nobody ever suggested that responsibility comes for free, and quite obviously some people sometimes handle it better than others.

Being stuck with the process doesn't mean, however, that we can't learn to do it better. In fact, I think the story of the moment is that we are being given endless opportunities to do just that. It may have appeared in our earlier discussion that the process of transformation and the work of grief take place only in mega-buster situations, when markets collapse, industries end, and organizations go out of business. While it is certainly easier to see the process in such extreme situations, I think the reality is that the precipitating events of transformation are occurring ever closer together. No longer are they separated by millennia, or even by the comfortable twenty-year cycle marked by the Generational Flush. Transformation is ongoing, and transformations lap at and pile on top of one another. We are quickly moving from the old slide presentation into the Great Organizational Picture Show.

In practical detail, this means that what was once a twenty-year or longer phenomenon, which we could afford to wait for and then hope to muddle through, is now an everyday occurrence. Unless we wish to be constantly surprised, we have the opportunity to handle it better. The opportunity is made richer by the fact that not only are major transformations coming with greater frequency, but there are a whole bunch of them going on all around us simultaneously, many of which we are hardly aware of.

What may be a precipitating event for you may be a matter of minor concern to me, and vice versa. So, for example, as president of a company it may make little existential difference to you that the product line for which I have given blood, sweat, and tears is about to be terminated. You see it as progress. For me, it is a disaster.

Sitting where I sit, it is the end of the world, or at least my world, which after all is the only one that counts for me. It is quite possible, indeed highly probable, that I will have a number of unkind things to say about you. That is called shock and anger. But I also have the opportunity to seize the particular moment as an occasion for evolution. Even more than that, I could also learn a great deal about the process, so the next time things fall apart, as surely they will, I will be ready.

The bottom line is quite simple. There was a day when the call for leadership came once a millennium, century, or decade. Leaders emerged to answer the call, and we judged them to be unique, awesome individuals. At the moment the call is going out constantly, so we all have the opportunity, and necessity, to try. Fortunately, I think the secret is out. The solitary leader is gone. We are all leaders.

NOTES

1. The seminal work in this area was done by Elisabeth Kübler-Ross, reported in her book *On Death and Dying* (New York: Collier Books, 1969).
2. *Whole, health,* and *holy* all share a common root, the Old English *hal.*
3. To say that transformation is a solo process might suggest that Organization Transformation is a nonreality. Indeed, there are

many who would argue that case and tell us to forget organization and deal only with individuals. The issue, in my view, is not individual versus organization but rather that neither fundamentally exists. What *is* is Spirit, which comes to form as individuals or (collectively) as organizations. The situation is not unlike that confronted by physicists relative to energy. For them, energy *is*, although one may choose to talk about it as either waves or particles. To ask which one is right is to invite the answer, "Whichever one is useful." We would all agree that no organization has ever existed without individuals, but I would suggest that the reverse is also true. We become who and what we are only in the context of our organizations, be they family, company, or country. A further discussion of this point can be found in my book *Spirit*.

CHAPTER 12

The Spirit of Leadership

The Leader's Spirit

I have an Indian friend and colleague who was the vice president for human resources of a large hotel group and is currently a consultant and university professor. Like many of his peers, my friend grew up in a Hindu family and, until the age of twelve or thirteen, went through what we might now call the consciousness-raising program common to the Hindus. He also participated in Western-style education through preparatory school and university. When he had completed his course of study, along with many others of his generation in India, he found the old ways somehow not in tune with the business environment of the late twentieth century. Quantitative methods, behavioral science, and a variety of other approaches had much more to do with the bottom line.

Then, for reasons that have never been shared with me, he made a remarkable discovery: as effective as his business school methods were in manipulating and interpreting the bottom line, the bottom line became positive and meaningful only in a context of inspired human performance. When Spirit was up, good things happened, and when it was not, no amount of number crunching was going to change the result. My friend realized what I have been suggesting here: Spirit is important.

My friend made another discovery: Spirit was not only important in general, but the quality of his own Spirit was critical to whatever he called his job. From this point came a final realization, that all those childish things that he put away shortly after reaching the age of thirteen were probably the most important foundations for his professional life.

My friend is not alone in his discovery. Some miles away, on the islands of Japan, a new leadership school has been established. Entry into the school, as in all schools in Japan, is a matter of fierce competition, for those who gain admission are expected to constitute a critical piece of Japanese leadership—corporate, governmental, and social. One might suspect that the old view of leadership is very much operative here, for the selection process is elitist in the extreme, but the program of the school is remarkable. It has four parts. Part One is Zen, Part Two is everything one might expect to receive in a good business school, Part Three involves a year-long journey to some other part of the world to see what is going on, and Part Four is a return home to ponder the significance of what has been experienced. It seems that matters of the Spirit are also primary to the Japanese.

In the United States and Western Europe one may gather an infinite number of similar stories. In some cases they describe a return to earlier religious traditions, when, as for my Indian friend, it is discovered that the childish things of long ago have striking new relevance to the present day. In other cases the tales relate explorations under a number of different banners, ranging from the Human Potential Movement to Transpersonal Psychology.

I am reminded of a seminar I held for a small number of Dutch executives in the mid 1980s. I was trying my best to gently edge the conversation into a consideration of transformation and Spirit. After about twenty minutes of going around the barn, Jean Pierre Guepin, the managing director of a global corporation, put up his hand with some impatience. "Stop, Harrison," he said, "We all know Spirit is important; the question is what to do with it." To a surprising extent I think that Guepin's premise has been accepted and we are now seriously about the business of dealing with his question.

So what can we say about the Spirit of leadership, or the leader's Spirit? First and most obviously, Spirit is the point of interconnection between us, in our leadership mode, and our fellows. *It is through our Spirit that we participate in the realm of Spirit.* This is our birthright, the commonality of our collective being, the basis from which all of us have not only the opportunity but also the responsibility to lead. It comes with our humanity.

There are, of course, a number of ways to ensure that the capacity for leadership remains stillborn. At the simplest level, we can deny the presence of Spirit and define our world exclusively in terms of the bits and pieces of our experience, the forms and structures that constitute everyday life. Such a definition locks life into its observable state, with predefined chains of command and levels of authority. In this case, only those at the top possess the necessary power and control to make a difference.

We may also abort the appearance of our unique leadership capacity by becoming enmeshed in the age-old discussion about the origin of leadership. Is it *nature* or *nurture*, born or made? The possibility of discussing this to death is a given, and should we resolve the issue in favor of nature and birth, we may find ourselves excused from the leadership role. I suggest that the distinction is false and that the answer is both. To the extent that we *are* and Spirit *is*, we have everything we need to begin. What happens after that is up to us. The capacity for leadership begins with our humanity, but it grows only with practice and intention.

There are no magic bullets or guarantees when it comes to developing our capacity to lead with Spirit. Four elements have appeared critical, however, in my experience: (1) learning about Spirit, (2) experiencing Spirit, (3) practicing leading with Spirit, and (4) reprise.

Learning About Spirit

I think it odd that some do not know the world of Spirit. This is awesome, for sure, but it is hardly strange, for the material on the subject is so voluminous as to boggle the mind. Indeed, I think the case can be made that until fairly recently, even in the West, virtually everything of substance, written or thought, had to do with Spirit, the manifestation of Spirit, or humankind's life as Spirit. If sometimes the subject has been approached obliquely or with unfamiliar language, I don't think the authors are to be blamed, and certainly cannot be faulted for lack of effort.

The inherent difficulty of the subject should not surprise us, for in truth it is hard to get mind and words around something that defies comprehension and transcends verbal description. It might be noted in passing that contemporary physicists have faced similar problems with comparable results. They have had the audacity to postulate a world that could neither be seen, touched, tasted, nor smelled—and then with outrageous persistence they have proceeded to describe it. To the uninitiated, the writings of the physicists seem bizarre to the extreme. The mysteries of mathematics aside, the thought that serious people would devote their lives to the study of odd beasties like quarks, neutrinos, and other inhabitants of the subatomic world is peculiar at best. Few, however, would dismiss the validity of the effort simply on the grounds that it is hard to understand.

The same may be said for Spirit and for the efforts of those who have made a life study of the subject. In truth we know an enormous amount about Spirit and its operation, but it takes real effort to assimilate that knowledge. In matters of the Spirit, those who refuse to do their homework will have a doubtful grasp of the subject.

Are we then to substitute the knowledge elite for the power elite? Yes, in the sense that there are guides who may be followed.

But also no, in the sense that the basis of this knowledge is somehow hidden from the general population. Unlike the physicists, we do not need to have access to a cyclotron or supercollider in order to join the club. Spirit is everywhere, available to anybody who chooses to be open to its presence. Furthermore, the basic manifestations of Spirit are simple in the extreme. We may see it in the lover's touch or in the grief of the bereaved. It does not take a graduate degree to perceive its presence. But when one comes to questions such as, What does it mean? Where is it going? and (to recall Jean Pierre Guepin), What do we do with it? We may do well to consult the work of those who have been there before.

All of which brings up the inevitable question, Where do we start? The answer is, basically, anywhere we like, and more usually, right where we are. You may discover, like my Indian friend, that your discarded tradition is, in fact, a valuable resource. To find out how valuable, you might try a little exercise in which you ask, What is it they (the Church fathers, rabbis, gurus, and so on) would have thought they were doing if they had thought what they were doing made sense? It often turns out that what we, in our youth, took to be idiotic obfuscation is actually quite useful.

In my own case, I don't think it will come as any surprise to reveal that virtually nothing written in this book is without precedent in the traditions of Christianity, Judaism, and their predecessors in the ancient Near East. The whole concept of griefwork assumed early form in the dying and rising god motifs from that area, which were subsequently reformulated in the story of the crucifixion for Christianity and of the exile for Israel. The story of Spirit has been around for a long time.

If your own tradition seems barren, try the tradition of another, perhaps from the Far East or the Native Americans; but don't be surprised if you find entry rather rough going. But then you wouldn't expect to understand quantum mechanics on your first day in class.

If you stay the course and don't give up the first time you run into an unpronounceable word, be prepared for an interesting surprise. As different as the several traditions may be, their similarities are often more striking. This fact was driven home in conversation with some of my Buddhist and Hindu colleagues, who at various times have accused me of reading deeply in their sacred traditions. Nothing could be further from the truth, for although I have read and benefited much, my real exposure is only a mile wide and an inch deep. The equation occurs not on the level of the traditions in question but rather in terms of what we all share: Spirit. So start anywhere you want, with a reasonable expectation of arrival at all other points.[1]

Experience Spirit

No book in the world can substitute for the experience of Spirit, and your opportunities to have that experience are limited only by your willingness to try.

Take any moment in time—this one, for example. Close your eyes, breath deeply, and imagine the face of one you love. Let the memories pass through, of all the places you went and the things you did. Don't hold on to any of these, just let them go. Concentrate on the face and let it be there. If you are not careful, you will encounter his or her Spirit. Stripped of time and space, elevated above the comings and goings of daily life, Spirit is. And beneath the Spirit of that person is a larger world of Spirit, which you may sense but not know. Try it. Spirit is available whenever we are available to it. It is not so much a matter of taking a lot of time but of having intention.

A silly mind game perhaps, but it is often necessary to trick the mind into stopping thinking, for thoughts more often than not get in the way of Spirit. Invoking Spirit, however, is not a party game, and although the little exercise I have just suggested may bring you to the edge of Spirit, it cannot substitute for more extended practice, which is what meditation (by whatever name or form) is all about.

At this point I can imagine some of you smiling knowingly as if to say, I knew it, sooner or later he was going to have us in the lotus position. Frankly, I can't get into the lotus position, and although it has proven useful for many generations of experienced Spirit watchers, it is not my cup of tea, nor do I believe that it is essential for the process. But disciplined practice is. Because there are any number of classes and teachers, usually no further away than your local church, synagogue, or temple, suggesting one or several is hardly the point. But if one does not work, do not despair; just keep your eyes open. Following the footprints of Spirit requires practice, and as any athlete knows, disciplined exercise is essential, but not all exercise forms are appropriate for you. Keep looking.

Given the fact that we live in a world seemingly bent on collective suicide, to say nothing of a business environment apparently out to destroy us, you may wonder how you can afford the apparent luxury of Spirit watching. I can only suggest that under the circumstances you can't afford *not* to. The next time you find yourself in the caldron of change—which is likely to be tomorrow morning—with responsibility for yourself and your colleagues, being able to intuit the flow of Spirit in others and to ground or center Spirit in yourself is likely to make the difference between realizing new opportunity and chalking up disaster. I don't think you can afford to be ill prepared.

Practice Leading

There is a general myth of powerlessness, and even such enlightened folks as the readers of this book are likely to fall prey. It is, after all, easier, more advisable, or appropriate to leave leadership to others, who can then assume the blame. We all do it, but I think you will agree that the time for such self-indulgence is rapidly running out.

Even when we have cast off the myth of powerlessness, the temptation is always to wait for the "Big One," that moment in history when the trumpets sound and we are called to the battlements. Unfortunately, when that moment arrives we are usually not ready. We must take the opportunity to practice leadership whenever and wherever we are.

For example, the next time a friend or colleague is "terminated," you will have the chance to be with them through shock, anger, memories, the dumps, and on into Open Space, imagination, and vision. Take the opportunity to practice creating space, and always ask questions. Check the flow of Spirit and see what happens if you start providing answers and not questions. Check your own Spirit for those telltale signs of anxiety that seemingly force you to exercise control.

Or let's say you are part of a secretarial pool or a small design team. For a while now you have been doing the same thing, and doing it very well—so well in fact that you actually enjoy what you are doing. Then one day, from the Olympian heights, comes the word: the group is through, the work is done. It's all over, baby. Guess what? You have another opportunity to help your fellows and yourself, while simultaneously enhancing your capacity for leadership. The occasion for practice is omnipresent, regardless of your perceived station in life. Whether you are on top of the heap or scarcely on the playing field, the opportunities are there.

And what does all this have to do with imminent global disaster? Nothing and everything. Quite obviously your friend's job loss or the demise of your working group will probably have minuscule impact on the global scene. But every time we practice and develop our innate capacity for leadership, it can only improve; so when the Big One does come, as it probably will, we will be ready. And when might that be? Who knows? Even the two young ladies at OCF could have had no premonition that they were going to exercise such a major role in the turnaround of Spirit in that place.

Yet even if the Big One never comes, practice is not in vain, for I think you will discover that as you enrich the Spirit of others, so your own Spirit will grow. And who knows, perhaps it is your role not to lead the charge but rather to feed the ball to those who will. Whoever has the ball is leader, but as we know by now, ball hogs die.

Reprise

As Rome was not built in a day, so our capacity for leadership is not brought to peak performance with a single iteration from learning to experience and on to practice. It is only when our practice of leadership is repetitively grounded in our learning, as enriched by our experience, that peak levels begin to emerge. There are no magic wands here, nor is there any cause for despair. The leadership we need is available in all of us. We have only to make it manifest.

NOTE

1. I have included in the bibliography a number of books that have been helpful to me. This is no guarantee that they will suit you. If you are looking for a place to start your own exploration of Spirit, however, these books may be useful.

SELECTED BIBLIOGRAPHY

The following are books that I have found to be interesting and useful. Some have had direct influence on the present book, but all have had an influence on me.

Bateson, Gregory. *Steps to an Ecology of Mind* (New York: Ballantine, 1972).

Buber, Martin. *I and Thou* (Clark, 1937).

Campbell, Jeremy. *Grammatical Man* (New York: Simon and Schuster, 1983).

Campbell, Joseph. *The Masks of God* (Vols. 1–4) (New York: Viking Penguin, 1962).

Campbell, Joseph. *The Hero with a Thousand Faces* (Princeton, N.J.: Princeton Press, 1949).

Capra, Fritjof. *The Tao of Physics* (New York: Bantam Books, 1980).

Cassirer, Ernst. *The Philosophy of Symbolic Forms* (Vols. 1–4) (New Haven, Conn.: Yale University Press, 1955).

Collingwood, R. G. *The Idea of History* (New York: Oxford University Press, 1946).

Coveney, Peter, and Highfield, Roger. *Frontiers of Complexity: The Search for Order in a Chaotic World* (New York: Ballantine, 1995).

Gleick, James. *Chaos: Making a New Science* (New York: Viking Penguin, 1987).

Grof, Stanislav. *Beyond the Brain: Birth, Death, and Transcendence in Psychotherapy* (Ithaca: State University of New York Press, 1985).

Hall, Edward T. *Beyond Culture* (New York: Anchor Books, 1977).

Hall, Edward T. *The Silent Language* (New York: Doubleday, 1959).

Heidegger, Martin. *On the Way to Language* (New York: HarperCollins, 1971).

Heidegger, Martin. *Being and Time* (New York: HarperCollins, 1962).

Henderson, Hazel. *Building a Win-Win World: Life Beyond Global Economic Warfare* (San Francisco: Berrett-Koehler, 1996).

Jaynes, Julian. *The Origin of Consciousness in the Breakdown of the Bicameral Mind* (Boston: Houghton Mifflin, 1976).

Jung, Carl G. *Symbols of Transformation* (Princeton, N.J.: Princeton University Press, 1956).

Kauffman, Stuart. *At Home in the Universe: The Search for Laws of Self-Organization and Complexity* (New York: Oxford University Press, 1995).

Kierkegaard, Soren. *Philosophical Fragments* (Princeton, N.J.: Princeton University Press, 1936).

Kübler-Ross, Elisabeth. *On Death and Dying* (New York: Collier Books, 1969).

Kuhn, Thomas. *The Structure of Scientific Revolutions* (Chicago: University of Chicago Press, 1962).

Laing, R. D. *The Politics of Experience* (New York: Ballantine Books, 1967).

Langer, Susanne K. *Philosophy in a New Key* (Cambridge, Mass.: Harvard University Press, 1982).

Lovelock, James E. *Gaia: A New Look at Life on Earth* (New York: Oxford University Press, 1979).

Maslow Abraham H. *Religions, Values, and Peak-Experiences* (New York: Viking Press, 1970).

Naisbitt, John. *Megatrends: Ten New Directions Transforming Our Lives* (New York: Warner Books, 1982).

Nielsen, Eduard. *Oral Tradition* (SCM Press, 1954).

Pedersen, Joseph. *Israel: Its Life and Culture* (New York: Oxford University Press, 1959).

Peters, Tom, and Waterman, Robert H. *In Search of Excellence* (New York: HarperCollins, New York, 1981).

Prigogine, Ilya. *Order Out of Chaos* (New York: Bantam Books, 1984).

Russell, Peter. *The Global Brain Awakens: Our Next Evolutionary Leap* (Los Angeles: Tarcher, 1983).

Toffler, Alvin. *The Third Wave* (New York: Morrow, 1980).

Vaill, Peter. "Towards a Behavioral Description of High Perform-ing Systems," in *Leadership: Where Else Can It Go?* Morgan McCall (ed.) (Durham, N.C.: Duke University Press, 1978).

Wilbur, Ken. *Up from Eden: A Transpersonal View of Human Evolution* (New York: Anchor Books, 1981).

Wilbur, Ken. *A Brief History of Everything* (Boston: Shambala, 1996).

Yankelovich, Daniel. *New Rules: Searching for Self-Fulfillment in a World Turned Upside Down* (Random House, 1981).

Young, Arthur M. *The Reflexive Universe: Evolution of Consciousness* (New York: Delacorte Press, 1977).

INDEX

Harrison Owen is president of H. H. Owen and Company. His academic background and training centered on the nature and function of myth, ritual, and culture. In the mid 1960s, he left academe to work with a variety of organizations, including small West African villages, urban community organizations (both in the United States and in Africa), the Peace Corps, regional medical programs, the U.S. National Institutes of Health, and the U.S. Veterans Administration. Along the way, he discovered that his study of myth, ritual, and culture had direct application to these social systems. In 1977, he created H. H. Owen and Company in order to explore the culture of organizations in transformation as a theorist and practicing consultant. Harrison Owen convened the First International Symposium on Organization Transformation and is the originator of Open Space Technology. He is the author of *Spirit: Transformation and Development in Organization; Riding the Tiger; Open Space Technology: A User's Guide; The Millennium Organization;* and *Tales from Open Space.*

Some of Harrison Owen's client engagements and presentations include the following organizations: Owens/Corning Fiberglas, Procter and Gamble, Dupont, Eastern Virginia Medical Authority, Shell/Netherlands, Shell Tankers (Dutch), Shell/

Canada, the French Ministry of Telecommunications (PTT), the U.S. Forest Service, the U.S. Internal Revenue Service, Jonathan Corporation, the U.S. Army, Ikea (Sweden), Statoil (Norway), SAS Airlines, Young Presidents Organization, City University Business School (London), Gronigen University Business School (Holland), Taj Hotel Group (India), Congresso de Desarrollo Organizacional (Mexico), PepsiCola (Venezuela), National Education Association, Toronto-Dominion Bank (Canada), American Management Systems, American Society of Training and Development, Scott Paper, TELCEL/Venezuela, the American Society of Association Executives, the Presbyterian Church (USA), the Accor Hotel Group (France), Ermetek Corp (South Africa), the Union of International Associations (Belgium), Rockport Shoes, Corporate Express, the World Bank, AT&T, IBM, U S WEST, the Organization Development Network, Lucent Technologies, and the Bank of Montreal.